INVESTING & FAITH

THE IMPACT OF FAITH-BASED INVESTING

CONTENTS

1

WHY FAITH-BASED INVESTING: AN INTRODUCTION

BY STEVE FRENCH

Faith-Based Investing? Socially responsible investing? Biblically responsible investing? Are they all terms of art—or is there a deeper meaning?

What does it mean to invest well? What does it mean to invest responsibly? Let me share some of my personal journey with you.

My career started in New York with Merrill Lynch. Like a lot of young guys, I had dreams of conquering the world. The days were long, but the work was fun and challenging. I helped my clients grow their portfolios and was rewarded in so many ways. I could have done this work forever!

Even though things were going great at Merrill and my career seemed to be on the fast track, I sensed God moving me to a different season. My boss thought I was nuts when I resigned my position.

After a season of intense training and experience in New York, I moved to Nashville by way of Memphis, where I put to work all I had learned about evaluating businesses. Through a private equity firm, I found the analysis and the challenge of investing in companies to be invigorating. It was even better to see those investments perform. Most of the models behind that work combined the science of measurable data from spreadsheets and proformas with the art of less measurable qualities of people and systems.

The learned discipline of investing in other companies led me to think I might be ready for a next step—a start-up business of my own. The first go at this was a collaboration of resources with some talented technology partners to launch one of the early internet service providers in Tennessee. That investment was at the right place and the right time. It proved to be quite successful and led me to a great first-start-up exit. If I'm really honest though, that exit probably gave me too much confidence.

Buoyed by that first venture, I decided I could invest in yet another technology start-up and become a dot-com entrepreneur. Unfortunately but providentially, the results were less than stellar. To be blunt, I failed and lost a lot of money. I tell people that business failure is where I earned my PhD in business. And looking back now, it was God's incredible love for me to receive the appropriate dose of humility that serves me well to this day.

Along the way, I found myself investing in other ventures. Sometimes it was real estate. Sometimes it was a friend's company. I was always looking for good returns and sought to do business with people I considered to be of great character. That endless curiosity led me to invest in yet another company.

That company was one of my longest ventures. We went from being a start-up to being a key player in the legal audit industry. I learned from the ground floor about building software. I also learned about investing in people. Business is never just about the process or the product, but it's about the people first.

That business provided me with some greater bandwidth, and in addition to investing in for-profit companies, I found myself investing in Kingdom opportunities. I was able to serve on the board of a nonprofit ministry that provided training to missionaries. I was captured by this work and ended up providing this ministry with office space in my building. From a business standpoint, some might have questioned the return on investment, but for me there was untold return for the Kingdom.

While it's a much longer story, my wife Debbie and I found ourselves investing in missions work in Africa. Before you think this was some noble effort, let me tell you I had no interest or desire in going to Africa. None. But I had some friends who tricked me into going. They relied on my real estate expertise, and they convinced me that I was the only one who could go and solve an existing problem for this ministry in Africa. I went, although I was dragging my feet. This trip opened my eyes to the developing world and its Kingdom needs in a way that changed my family forever!

Over the next 20 years, I found myself in Africa at least once a year. To this day, some of the best relationships and warmest memories of my life came out of our investment in that ministry effort.

Ultimately, I exited my legal audit business after 18 years of hard work. But this time I promised my wife that I'd sit on the sidelines for six months and just listen to what the Lord would have for me. So I did. Patiently. Actually, not really *patiently*, but it felt good to write it that way.

Mind you, after a successful exit, I had other firms offering me lots of opportunities. But once again, I sensed the Lord leading me to make a Kingdom investment. Some might call it "Faith-Based Investing." I stumbled across the work of Bill High at The Signatry, and I was inspired by the vision of growing generosity to advance the Great Commission around the globe.

That seemed like a great investment—an incredible investment in fact. So my wife and I prayed and decided to invest the next season of our lives with The Signatry. Soon thereafter, we began to see incredible things happen—an outpouring of generosity in Nashville and beyond. The board and Bill asked me to step up and become the president of The Signatry.

In that role, we were able to launch a new donor advised fund platform that would allow us to offer lower fees and allow advisors to manage from first dollar. But equally important, we found that we could provide a biblically responsible investment platform or what some call a faith-based investment platform. I was surprised by the response of those in the Christian investment community. There was a pent-up demand for something cutting edge yet with great performance.

We continue to be amazed by the opportunity. So back to the question: Why Faith-Based Investing? Why biblically responsible investing?

I think it is so much like my journey — and the journey we are all on. We want to have our actions align with our values.

That sounds pretty simple—actions aligning with values. But for me it's been an evolving journey.

My Merrill Lynch season taught me that it was more than just making money. And my private equity season taught me not only the importance of systems and processes but also the intangible and incredible value of people. My business successes and failures taught me the incredible lesson of success balanced with humility. And my long-term business run of 18 years perhaps prepared me for how my business needed to be aligned with my Kingdom investments. For only one of these will last.

In the coming pages, you'll learn from experts in the field of Faith-Based Investing. Our hope is that this learning and growth will contribute to your own journey. In whatever way God leads each of us, let's be successful Kingdom investors.

2

FAITH-BASED INVESTING: A HISTORY

BY ART ALLY

You don't have to be a Christian to want to invest your money in companies that make the world a better—not a worse—place. But Christians and Jews have additional insight through the Scriptures that all our money—and our time—belongs to God, not just the money we tithe or the time we spend in worship.

Christians and Faith-Based Economics

Throughout history, Christians have promoted one form or another of biblically responsible economic activity. In 1524, Christian reformer Martin Luther excoriated businessmen who left out ethics:

"The merchants have a common rule ...I shall sell my wares as dear as I can ... But it means making room for greed and opening the door and window of hell. So long as I have my profit and satisfy my greed, of what concern is it to me if it injures my neighbor in ten ways at once? So you see how this motto goes so straight and shamelessly against not only Christian love but also natural law as well."[1]

John Wesley (1703-1791), the founder of the Methodist movement, "urged his followers to shun profiting at the expense of their neighbors. Consequently, they avoided partnering or investing with those who earned their money through alcohol, tobacco, weapons, or gambling —essentially establishing social investment screens."[2]

Before the United States became an independent nation, English-born New Jersey tailor John Woolman (1720-1772) refused to buy any cotton or dye handled by slaves. "What pious Man could be a Witness to these Things, and see a Trade carried on in this Manner, without being deeply affected with Sorrow?" he wrote. "Through abiding in the Love of Christ, we feel a Tenderness in our Hearts toward our Fellow Creatures entangled in oppressive Customs; and a Concern so to walk that our Conduct may not be a Means of strengthening them in Error. It was the Command of the Lord through Moses, '*Thou shalt not suffer Sin upon thy Brother*.'"[3]

In 1759, Woolman persuaded the Quakers in Philadelphia to pass the first resolution in the colonies prohibiting participation in any aspect of the slave trade, presaging the Abolitionist Movement that led to the Civil War (1861-1865).[4]

Faith-Based Investing in the 20th Century

In 1928 Philip Carret launched the Fidelity Mutual Trust, which became the Pioneer Fund, one of the first-ever mutual funds. Designed initially to serve church investors, the Fund had a policy of "screening investments on ethical grounds," rejecting companies that traded in alcohol or tobacco. The Fund survived the Great Depression and went on to become one of the largest mutual funds. Recalling Carret, who died at age 101 in 1998, Warren Buffet said, "Phil was a hero of mine. He had the best long-term investment record of anyone I know."[5]

In 1976 Larry Burkett founded Christian Financial Concepts, teaching people biblical financial management as part of a larger life plan. In 2000 CFC merged with Crown Ministries, founded by Howard Dayton in 1985. Crown Financial, based in Knoxville, Tennessee, encourages people to get out of debt and live within strict budgets, just as radio host and financial ministry leader Dave Ramsey does.

In 1989 Tom Strobhar, a pro-life investment advisor in Dayton, Ohio, began buying a few shares in 25 corporations so he could attend stockholder meetings and lobby management against donating to Planned Parenthood, investing in pornography, or promoting immoral lifestyles. "Folks like Timothy Plan have made [abortion] an issue, so it has worked," Mr. Strobhar said in an interview, noting that at least 340 companies that formerly gave to Planned Parenthood have ceased doing so.[6] Mr. Strobhar authored the first shareholder resolutions against child pornography, religious bigotry, fetal tissue research, and abortifacient drugs.[7]

In January 1994, MMA Praxis Mutual Funds, designed with Mennonite beliefs, sought companies that support positive values such as the respect for human dignity, responsible management, and environmental stewardship, while avoiding industries and activities like gambling, alcohol and tobacco production, and military contracting.[8] Also, in 1994 some Catholic investment advisors opened the LKCM Aquinas Fund, "which focuses on issues such as race and gender equality, environmental practices, and human rights," according to Forbes.[9]

Faith-Based Biblical Blueprint

The field of Faith-Based Investing (FBI) is not really new; God gave us the blueprint from the very beginning. The current application just happens to revolve around modern investment opportunities.

Genesis 1 through 3 tells us that God created all things, including men and women, for His own glory and that human beings are at the very top of His creative order. This means human beings, while inherently sinful, are beloved by God and should be treated with dignity, respect, and compassion. So everything we do, including our investments, needs to take that into account. We should vigorously avoid ventures that traffic in sin and thus are destructive to people.

This kind of stewardship begins with the acknowledgement of who is the real Chairman of the Board: "I believe the most dangerous misconception is the idea our money and possessions belong to us, not God," says Randy Alcorn, author and founder of Eternal Perspective Ministries. "Many of our problems begin when we forget that God is the Boss of the universe. But in fact, He is more than the Boss; He is the Owner."[10]

From beginning to end, Scripture repeatedly emphasizes God's ownership of everything: "To the Lord your God belong the heavens, even the highest heavens, the earth and everything in it" (Deuteronomy 10:14). When I grasp that I'm a steward, not an owner, it totally changes my perspective.

Suddenly, I'm not asking, "How much of my money shall I, out of the goodness of my heart, give to God?" Rather, I'm asking, "Since all of 'my' money is really yours, Lord, how would you like me to invest your money today?"

The importance of our money management is also reflected in many Bible passages. There are more than 2,300 verses that mention money—more than any other topic, including faith (500 verses)—so God cares deeply about what we do with money. Scripture often reminds us that, although money is important, our earthly and eternal security lies in our relationship with God.

"And you shall remember the Lord your God, for it is He who gives you power to get wealth, that He may establish His covenant which He swore to your fathers, as it is this day" (Deuteronomy 8:18).

"And my God shall supply all your need according to His riches in glory by Christ Jesus" (Philippians 4:19).

Additionally, the Bible places much importance on how wealth is accumulated. "Better is a little with righteousness, than vast revenues without justice" (Proverbs 16:8). Jesus Himself put it most starkly: "For what profit is it to a man if he gains the whole world and loses his own soul?" (Matthew 16:26)

Timothy Plan Story

This is my story and my reasons for launching the first Faith-Based mutual fund that screened out companies involved in abortion and pornography. Because of my strong belief in the infallible Word of God and the 25 years of being blessed in this space, it would not seem fitting to dismiss the importance of being biblically responsible. For that reason, I would like to focus on biblically responsible investing (BRI) as a category within Faith-Based Investing, specifically for Christians who desire to be biblical stewards of the assets God has given them.

In 1992 I had a very nice practice going in Orlando (Covenant Financial Management) and a 14-year career as a financial consultant and branch manager, but I felt called by God to make a change. I was very active in the pro-life community but wanted to do much more for God's Kingdom.

My hot button was the fact that, while pastors in denominations often had decent retirement plans, the pastors from independent churches were left high and dry. So I began to put together a retirement program geared to helping them on a national scale.

I soon realized that I could not use companies that trafficked in sin when these pastors were preaching against the evils of abortion and pornography from the pulpits. I looked around for a system that would screen out offenders and allow for building biblically responsible portfolios, not only for pastors but also for other Christian investors. But I found little that reflected biblical principles. A few socially screened funds excluded alcohol and tobacco, but none screened for issues such as abortion and pornography.

After two years of research and development, in March 1994 we launched the Timothy Plan, a mutual fund based on a founding commitment that we would never compromise biblical principles. We have been true to that vision throughout, and I believe that's why God has allowed us to proceed and grow.

My wife Bonnie came up with the Timothy Plan name, based

on two Scripture verses from 1 Timothy:

"But if anyone does not provide for his own, and especially for those of his household, he has denied the faith and is worse than an unbeliever" (5:8).

"Do not lay hands suddenly on anyone, and do not partake of other men's sins. Keep yourself pure" (5:22).

These concepts—financial responsibility and spiritual discretion—have guided the Timothy Plan.

"Not a Penny"

Our arrival was not met with universal enthusiasm. "This fund may have gone too far. It sounds like someone trying to preach to the converted and then setting up a big collection," mutual fund analyst Michael Lipper told Bloomberg News.[11]

My Wall Street friends all told me that what I intended to do was impossible. "You can't do that, take out some of the most profitable companies, and expect to make any money," they'd say. But my answer to them was that, in God's economy, obedience trumps performance every time.

Besides, you don't even have to sacrifice performance. We are competitive. At times we trail, and we're at a comparative disadvantage when stocks run wild. But over time, it evens out, and we are competitive in the long run.

I found out early who was the real Chairman of the Board. It wasn't me. We needed to raise $1 million in capital to get the fund going, so I formed Timothy Partners, Ltd. and made a list of 50 well-to-do friends who could invest $50,000 without really missing it. That meant I only needed to find 20 people. But I didn't even find 20. Only three came aboard, but they provided enough capital to get us started.

That told me that I only thought I knew who should have been in the group but that God knew all along how many people it would take. Over the next six months, I met people I had never known before who became initial investors, and we raised the full million. We found a Philadelphia firm to handle shareholder investment services, such as accounting, and we were off and running with a single small cap value fund.

The original board of trustees for the Timothy Plan consisted of Mark Schweizer (Trustee), Gregory F. Tighe (Executive Vice President/Secretary), Dr. J. C. Mitchell (Treasurer), Wesley W. Pennington (Trustee), and me as president.

Our first marketing piece concealed a penny with the following question: "How much money is okay to have invested in abortion or pornography?" The answer is simple. "Not a penny."

The Timothy Plan initially focused on five major factors: abortion, pornography, alcohol, tobacco, and casino gambling. Later, we added screens for anti-family entertainment and alternative lifestyles to the mix. Our screens of gambling, tobacco, and alcohol may be areas where a certain element of "Christian liberty" could be expressed, but because of the overwhelming abuses and destruction caused to society, we screen them.

In 1995 we helped launch eVALUEator, a screening service for advisors. This service identifies companies actively involved in, profiting from, or financially supporting any one of the target areas. Though we limit our screening to eight categories, there are many sub-screens that trigger violations. For example, our abortion screen consists of sub-screened categories such as abortifacients, cloning,

fetal stem-cell research, and donations to organizations like Planned Parenthood.

Early Struggles

Business was very slow at first. We began losing $40,000 or $50,000 each month, despite the fact that our materials and operation were of a quality that would rival Merrill Lynch. In 18 months we ran out of money. It was the lowest point of my life. All these people had trusted me with their money, and it was gone. I went back to a few of the partners who agreed to inject some more money into the operation, and it carried us for a little while, but growth was still painfully slow.

We frankly had difficulty attracting investors because of the typical Christian view that business is business and church is church. Over the next eight years, we ran out of money four times.

I asked God, "Why aren't people investing with us?" and got a clear answer: "Because they don't know and are not being taught." I looked around for teaching resources, but there was nothing that pulled it all together.

So I told my wife Bonnie that I was going to write a course and guidebook on comprehensive stewardship. I asked Randy Alcorn to help with writing. He was too busy writing his own book, but he did give us permission to use his excellent material, as did Howard Dayton of Crown Financial Ministries.

It took me three months to assemble what became *Stewardship: God's Plan for Financial Success*, first published in 2004, a work which my daughter Cheryl updates regularly. We also put together a family edition study guide with the help of financial planning professionals Dan Hardt, Mark Henry, Todd Sadowski, Paul Saxton, Charles Schultz, and C. Buck Stephens. Mat Staver of Liberty Counsel contributed the chapter on cultural stewardship.

Over the years the going was rough, but every time we were in trouble God led me to people that He wanted to be part of our mission. The last time we were out of money was New Year's Eve in 2002. We had a 4 p.m. deadline to come up with the cash or be put out of business by the Securities and Exchange Commission. We all prayed. And prayed. And prayed. And just before 4 p.m., the phone rang, and it was an investor who came up with the money.

I knew then that I could be comfortable trusting God, since He could have shut us down anytime in the preceding eight years. Instead, He forced us through a keyhole four times. The lesson is that we can trust God—and He has to know that He can trust us.

"Let Me Get This Straight—You Want to Do What?"

At one point, we realized that we needed to raise money to launch Class B shares, which pay a sales commission of 4% of the amount that financial advisors invest for their clients in our funds. We learned that Class B funds do not normally finance themselves; they are financed through banks and credit. We applied at a bank for a credit line of $1 million, which was a pretty audacious thing to do. The loan officer looked at our application and shook his head. After all, most of the loans from that bank involved rock-solid real estate deals. We, on the other hand, had no history, and the company

16

behind the new venture was losing money. But he agreed to present the proposal and came back saying something like, "You're not going to believe this, but they approved it."

We needed money managers and went to UBS Institutional in Atlanta to make our case. The fellow we spoke to said, "Let me get this straight: You want to do what? You have no money. You're starting with some major stocks excluded. And your fee schedule is less than these money managers' largest clients. And you want them to come aboard the Timothy Plan?" Yes, we did. And they did. These UBS consultants even worked for free at first to help get us off the ground.

Now, can you tell me that God's hand was not in all of this? I must reiterate: I am not in charge of this company. Jesus is the Chairman of the Board.

From then on, we started growing and have not stopped. On July 20, 2018, we hit a milestone with $1 billion in assets under management and now manage 13 mutual funds.

A Growing Field

As the Timothy Plan matured, others joined the FBI movement. In December 1997 I announced the formation of the National Association of Christian Financial Consultants to provide a forum for Christian advisors to come together, worship, and figure out how to change investors' ideas about investing. I served as president from 1998 to 2001. In 2005, the Association created the Christian Financial Consultant and Advisor (CFCA)® certification training program.

In 2005, the Timothy Plan absorbed the Noah Fund, which was founded in 1996 as a mutual fund based on Judeo-Christian principles and which invested only with "what we believe is a moral, spiritual, and ethical standard, but also with an emphasis on low risk, high growth stocks."[12] That fund tithed 10% of management earnings to "missions and the needs of the poor."[13]

In 1997 Larry Burkett brought together 16 friends and professionals to form the Christian Financial Planning Institute (CFPI). In 2003, these men and women created a new organization for outreach to the Christian financial professional community. The Christian Financial Professionals Network (CFPN) under the leadership of Ron Blue began to grow and in 2007 was renamed Kingdom Advisors.[14]

In 2000 former Templeton Global portfolio manager and analyst Howard "Rusty" Leonard founded Stewardship Partners and began managing money in separately managed accounts (SMAs) from a Christian worldview perspective. While still at Templeton, Mr. Leonard and his wife Carol developed Wall Watchers, a ministry designed to help Christians be better stewards of their giving.[15]

"SMAs differ from pooled vehicles, like mutual funds, in that each portfolio is unique to a single account (hence the name). If you set up a separate account with Money Manager X, then Manager X has the discretion to make decisions for this account that may be different from decisions made for other accounts."[16]

A large Catholic firm, Ave Maria Funds, was launched in 2001. "The fund's managers generally adhere to a socially conservative bent that excludes companies involved with abortion, contraception, or pornography as well as companies that offer domestic partner benefits." [17]

In 2012 the Christian Investment Forum (CIF) was formed

in Charlotte, North Carolina, as a "Kingdom-focused investment association committed to educating advisors and investors by providing opportunities to bring about change—in the hearts, homes, cities, nation, and world that we serve." The CIF has 11 member firms: Advisor Solutions 360, Beacon Wealth, Camelot Mutual Fund, Creative Financial Design Investments, Epiphany Funds, Eventide, Guidestone, In His Steps (IHS) Foundation, Praxis Mutual Funds, Sage Stone Wealth Management, and the Timothy Plan.[18]

Other faith-based mutual funds reflect the values of Baptist, Lutheran, Presbyterian, Mennonite and evangelical denominations. "The largest group in terms of assets is Guidestone Funds, which has more than $7 billion in assets spread across 23 funds, including five target-date funds," Forbes reports. Guidestone avoids investing in companies that are publicly perceived to be involved in alcohol, tobacco, gambling, pornography, or abortion.[19]

The Rise of FBI Financial Advisors

As the field grew, more Christian financial advisors began screening for biblically sound investments. Some offered a stewardship-based approach even before the advent of Faith-Based Investing screening tools.

In Kokomo, Indiana, Mick L. Owens, who began his career in financial services in 1969, founded the Creative Financial Centre that year with a network of associates "committed to serving clients in the Christ-like manner by assisting them in development of stewardship in their lives."[20]

Among the most prominent FBI pioneer advisors was Glenn A. Repple of Florida-based G.A. Repple & Company. He is an independent financial planner operating under the principles of biblically responsible investing. Mr. Repple is a certified teacher of biblical entrepreneurship and has trained more than 600 business leaders who have likewise spread the FBI principles into 23 countries.[21]

Other prominent leaders include Daniel L. Hardt of Dan Hardt Financial Services in Louisville, Kentucky. When he served as president of the National Association of Christian Financial Consultants, he popularized the phrase Faith-Based Investing in his public speaking.[22]

Mark Minnella is another major figure in the FBI movement. In 2002, he founded Integrity Investors, LLC, a St. Louis-based company, to align his clients' investments with their biblical beliefs. A co-founder of the National Association of Christian Financial Consultants, Inc., Mark designed the first biblically responsible, faith-based professional designation program, Christian Financial Consultant and Advisor and served on the Timothy Plan Board of Trustees.[23]

Comparable Returns

The most important reason for biblically responsible, Faith-Based Investing is to honor God by aligning the shareholders' investments with their values. But a growing body of research indicates that investors do not have to hurt their bottom lines while doing so and may even reap higher returns in some cases.

For example, in 2015 a Christian Investment Forum study noted that, "Based on the analysis of historical performance data from the funds managed by members of the Christian Investment Forum [of which the Timothy Plan is a participant], the results did, in fact, corroborate the expectation that return performance was not reduced due to incorporating BRI, and in fact there was a general outperformance compared to the industry averages. Over the last 5 years, a composite of the returns from all of the equity mutual funds within the Christian Investment Forum outperformed the industry average by 77 basis points (bp) on an annualized basis."[24]

Summary

Nearly $16 trillion is invested in mutual funds, and about 68% of that is held by Christians.[25] Christians also hold 41% of all money invested in securities.[26] Many activist movements represent a tiny fraction of the population. With less than 1% of our population effecting change within our nation in some areas, imagine the possible impact of Christians investing with purpose beyond monetary return. We could change the world.

Christians in America have been blessed beyond measure to be living in a self-governing, prosperous nation in which we're free to worship according to our conscience and to practice our faith. It's not unreasonable to allocate our resources, including our time and finances, in ways that bring glory to God and encourage biblical values in our culture.

Put simply, we need to put our money where it advances our faith. In God's economy, we must consider not only investments that bring a healthy return but also outcomes that our money facilitates. However, most people don't have the time or expertise to sort out the market, which is why trusted biblically responsible Faith-Based Investing financial advisors are so important.

In a sermon about the proper uses of money, John Wesley said this:

I. We ought to gain all we can gain, but this it is certain we ought not to do: we ought not to gain money at the expense of life, nor at the expense of our health.

II. Do not throw the precious talent into the sea.

III. Having first gained all you can and secondly saved all you can, then give all you can.[27]

The Bottom Line:

You can't give if you haven't got. Now we can earn returns on our money without being vested in things that are contrary to the love and mission of Christ. With the options available today and the knowledge of those options, you're either working for God or against Him. God enables us to allocate His resources, but it is our responsibility to allocate funds in a way that honors God.

References:

1. Martin Luther. (19150 Price fixing by commission. In W. H. Hamilton (Ed.), Current economic problems: A series of readings in the control of industrial development (p. 158). Chicago, IL: The University of Chicago Press.
2. William Donovan. (February 7, 2018). A short history of socially responsible investing. The Balance. Retrieved from http://www.thebalance.com/a-short-history-of-socially-responsible-investing-3025578
3. John Woolman. (1922). On the slave trade. In A. M. Gummere (Ed.) The journal and essays of John Woolman, (pp. 496-503). Retrieved from http://www.qhpress.org/texts/oldqwhp/wool-496.
4. Ibid.
5. Bud Labitan. (2014). The four filters invention of Warren Buffett and Charlie Munger, p. 178.
6. Tom Strobhar. (2018, March 13). Telephone interview with Robert

Knight.

7. Thomas Strobhar Financial. (n.d.). About. Retrieved from http://www.strobharfinancial.org/about.htm.

8. Securities and Exchange Commission. (2006, May 1). MMA Praxis Mutual Funds 485APOS prospectus. Retrieved from www.sec.gov.

9. LKCM Aquinas Catholic Equity Fund. (n.d.) Who we are. Retrieved from www.aquinasfunds.com/ wp-content/uploads/2018/01/LKCM-Aquinas-Catholic-Equity-Fund-4Q17.pdf

10. Randy Alcorn. (2017, July 5). Christ-centered stewardship in a consumer-driven culture: An interview about money and giving. Eternal Perspective Ministries. Retrieved from https://www.epm.org/blog/2017/Jul/5/christ-centered-stewardship

11 Bloomberg Business News. (1994, April 15). New fund seeks Christians. The News Journal.

12. The Noah Fund. (n.d.). Internet Archive Wayback Machine. Retrieved from www.noahfund.com:80

13. Ibid.

14. Kingdom Advisors. (n.d.). History. Retrieved from http://www.kingdomadvisors.com/about/history.

15. Stewardship Partners. (n.d.). Our history. Retrieved from stewardshippartners.com/about.htm

16. Katrina Lamb. (2018, January 24). Separately managed accounts: A mutual fund alternative. Investopedia. Retrieved from www.investopedia.com/articles/mutualfund/08/ managed-separate-account.asp

17. David K. Randall. (2009, May 22). Easy ways to invest based on your faith. Forbes. Retrieved from www.forbes.com/2009/05/22/faith-mutual-funds-moneybuilder-personal-finance-religious-investing.html#35ed16558844

18. Christian Investment Forum. (n.d.). Home page. Retrieved from https://christianinvestmentforum.org/

19. Op cit. Randall, Forbes.

20. Creative Financial Centre. (n.d.). About us. Retrieved from http://http://www.cfdinvestments.com/Investors/about.html

21. G. A. Repple. (n.d.). About. Retrieved from www.garepple.com

22. Dan Hardt (2018, March 13). Telephone interview with Robert Knight.

23. Mark Minnella (2018 January 26). Telephone interview with Robert Knight.

24. John Siverling (2015, May). A research study on CIF member

funds composite performance relative to industry averages (Christian Investment Forum white paper), p. 2. Retrieved from www.christianinvestmentforum.org/ content/uploads/2015/06/CIF-Study-on-BRI- Funds-Performance-Spring-2015.pdf

25. Investment Company Institute. (2015). 2015 investment company fact book (55th ed.) Washington, D.C.: Investment Company Institute. Retrieved from www.ici.org

26. Pew Research Center. (2014). Religious landscape study. Retrieved from www.pewforum.org

27. John Wesley. (n.d.). The use of money, sermon 50, John Wesley sermons, the United Methodist Church, 1872. (The text for John Wesley's sermons originally came from the Christian Classics Ethereal Library). Retrieved from http://www.umcmission.org/Find-Resources/John-Wesley-Sermons/Sermon-50-The-Use-of-Money

3

THE CURRENT STATE OF FAITH-BASED INVESTING

BY CASSANDRA LAYMON
& HILLARY SUNDERLAND

When Faith-Based Investing first came on the scene, there were many advisors who were excited about the possibility of choosing investments that would honor God. They understood that being an investor meant being an owner of a company and that investment in business practices that harm others not only profits from those activities but also promotes them.

While we in the Christian community would, of course, strive to honor God with our investments, there were also advisors who perceived this to be an impractical or legalistic approach. They were concerned that they would have to abandon the sound fundamentals of investing and accept higher fees and poor performance if they were to choose these investments.

A significant challenge to investing according to biblical

principles is that historically there has been a lack of sufficient products for advisors to utilize. This presents a "chicken and the egg" problem because fund companies don't want to develop a product unless there's a demand, and we can't create a demand until we have the products.

We are excited to share that we are entering an era where the concerns of advisors on both sides of the issue are presently being resolved. This creates a unique opportunity for financial advisors in the body of Christ to come together and invest in a way that makes a difference by defunding business practices we oppose while channeling those funds to great companies we support and admire.

Being a Good Steward Means Being a Fiduciary to Our Clients

Some financial advisors have assumed in recent decades that Faith-Based Investing (or any other screening mandate) is somehow in conflict with being a proper fiduciary for clients.

In its infancy, Faith-Based Investing options tended to be more expensive, and performance sometimes tended to lag.

Investopedia says this about what it means to be a fiduciary: "A fiduciary's responsibilities or duties are both ethical and legal. When a party knowingly accepts a fiduciary duty on behalf of another party, he or she is required to act in the best interest of the principal, the party whose assets they are managing. The fiduciary is expected to manage the assets for the benefit of the other person rather than for his or her own profit and cannot benefit personally from their management of assets."[1]

As Christians, we add to this legal definition the obligation to be good stewards of all God has entrusted to us. Colossians 3:23 says, "Whatever you do, work heartily, as for the Lord and not for men." If we look at the way we invest as working for the Lord, we realize that this is indeed a sacred responsibility. In an effort to serve in all of these roles, many advisors have decided to focus on the legal aspects of being a fiduciary to their client and to forgo any kind of screening. But this view results in advisors missing out on the opportunity to serve their clients on a deeper level.

Here's what that approach misses: In a survey conducted by the Christian Investment Forum, nearly 80% of Christian investors have expressed an interest in Faith-Based Investing.[2] However, there is still a big awareness gap and an opportunity for the advisors: 77% of respondents said an advisor had never spoken with them about values-based investing.[3]

In another study released by Morgan Stanley, a total of 75% of individual investors expressed interest in achieving social impact with their investment dollars. Twenty-three percent were "very interested," and 52% were "somewhat interested." When advisors were asked the same question, only 9% were "very interested," and 31% purported to be "somewhat interested."

Interest in Achieving Social Impact Through Investments

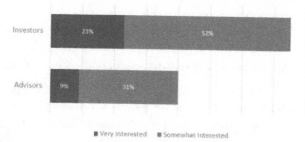

■ Very Interested   ■ Somewhat Interested

Source: Morgan Stanley Institute for Sustainable Investing, Sustainable Signals: New Data from the Individual Investor, 2017

If less than one-quarter of investors have heard about values-based investing from their advisors, it certainly seems that advisors are missing an opportunity to introduce this offering to their clients. Clearly, many clients want their investments to be more than just ticker symbols on a page. They want to make a difference with their investment dollars. They just need advisors to show them how. We believe in the importance of having these values conversations with clients. This means exploring the importance of our clients' values being reflected in their portfolios as part and parcel of our duty as fiduciaries.

When building a portfolio, advisors should look at the fundamentals, including reasonable fees; risk/return characteristics of the fund such as alpha, beta and Sharpe ratios; and of course, proper diversification so the portfolio performs well in a variety of market and economic environments. It's important to emphasize that these criteria should not be abandoned.

A challenge that we have faced in the Faith-Based Investing space is the limited number of products that are available, making it difficult to create fully asset-allocated portfolios. Faith-Based Investing funds tend to tilt towards mid-cap and small-cap companies, which can go out of favor in some market environments, and many strategies are very growth oriented. It has been a challenge to create a portfolio that has exposure to most segments of the market.

Advisors who are passionate about Faith-Based Investing may have been tempted in the past to overlook the fundamentals in favor of screening because we most certainly want to honor God with our investments. If advisors select only the most stringently screened, Faith-Based Investing funds, they may be excluding asset classes in their allocations. As a result, there are certain market environments that can hurt the risk/return profile over time.

This has caused some advisors to be understandably reluctant to create Faith-Based Investing portfolios for their clients. They are concerned about potential negative performance and don't want to take the risk of not acting in the best interest of the client. They may even go so far as to think it irresponsible to overlook the fundamentals in favor of screened investments.

The good news is that several research studies show that when companies are excluded from a portfolio for values alignment, the performance of the portfolio is not statistically different than a non-screened portfolio.[4]

Negative Screening

On the other end of the spectrum, there are advisors who are passionate about portfolio screening. Those who are familiar with the idea of values-based investing know that negative screening is of high importance. Business practices that we would like to avoid—in this case because of biblical principles—are identified and securities excluded from a portfolio. Some examples of these business practices are abortion, abortion philanthropy (contributions to Planned Parenthood and similar organizations), pornography and adult entertainment, and any industry that preys on addictive behaviors such as alcohol, tobacco, and gambling.

This sounds like an admirable and very straightforward approach! However, as advisors become savvier about the screening tools that are available and their methodologies, it becomes an increasingly complex challenge to fulfill this goal. Why is it difficult to completely remove these companies from a portfolio? Today, companies are involved in many business practices. Some of their business lines may be aligned with faith-based values; others may be in opposition to them. Staying informed requires a screening service (or several) that will provide that data.

Those who employ screening services know that results can vary from one service to another. Let's look at two well-respected screening companies—eVALUEator and ENSOGO Analytics.

There are well-known funds that score as a 0% failure rate in eVALUEator but a 20% failure rate in ENSOGO Analytics. Likewise, there are funds that can screen less than a 10% failure rate in ENSOGO but have a 30% failure rate in eVALUEator. If we were to use just one screening service, we may unnecessarily exclude a very good investment manager from our portfolios. It's easy to see how this can be problematic for advisors who are trying to build their own portfolios.

Given the complexity of screening, the decision process is becoming more of a discernment process than a binary "if this, then that" process. Some important questions that advisors need to address include:

- What is the fund supposed to be doing by prospectus?

- Is the fund following that mandate?

- Does the fund still show failures in our various screening providers?

- When comparing sources of information from the screening providers, are the failures explainable?

Considering what is available from a risk/return standpoint

in this particular asset class, what is the most prudent choice given our dual mandate of proper investment management and sound stewardship?

In the world of Faith-Based Investing, striving for perfectionism can prevent us from making great decisions that will positively impact the Kingdom. Perfectionism encourages us to have an all-or-nothing approach to investing—if I can't screen a portfolio to be 100% "clean," then I'm not going to do it at all. We are moving into an era where advisors are taking more responsibility for really understanding the screens and focusing on the heart of what we want to achieve rather than taking a legalistic approach.

We believe that advisors who are waiting for the perfect Faith-Based Investing portfolio to come along will miss out on some great opportunities to help our clients apply faith-based screening to their investments. Here are three great reasons not to wait to get started:

1. There simply are no perfect funds. What one service screens as perfect may be found lacking by another (therefore, we currently utilize three different screening data providers). Investing in funds and portfolios that are managed diligently, although not yet up to the desired standards, is helping to move the Faith-Based Investing space in a positive direction. If we show no interest in a fund before it is ideal, it's difficult for fund companies and money managers to realize there is a market demand for their products.

By taking small steps, we demonstrate encouragement and support, and we can be influencers for managers to hear our ideas about what we'd like to see in the way of screening criteria. As we start to do that, we'll be blessed with more and more competitive products. Progress, not perfection! "Whoever can be trusted with very little can also be trusted with much…" (Luke 16:10).

2. It's hard to meet all the requirements for appropriate asset allocation, reasonable fees, and risk-adjusted performance from the very few funds that screen clean using a particular screening tool. Besides being biblically responsible, we must also follow the fiduciary standards of our industry in terms of providing cost-conscious and well-performing portfolios to our clients. In the case where certain style boxes cannot be filled, we look for the best screened option available in that category.

3. There are many areas of life in which we must take the best course of action, even if the outcome is less than perfect. In other contexts, this all-or-nothing mindset seems silly. For instance, if I can't insulate my house to protect from all heat loss, should I bother to insulate it at all? If all food that I eat cannot be completely healthy for my body, should I even bother to monitor the nutritional value of any of it? Until I completely clean up my act, why/how can I become a Christian? Of course, we want to insulate our homes and nourish our bodies and souls to the best extent possible. Likewise, investing in that which is as righteous as it can be makes a big impact in our world for the better, even if we cannot screen out every violation.

Positive Screening

Over the last few years, there has been a fresh movement in the Faith-Based Investing space focused on positive screening. This concept was popularized by Eventide Asset Management and its "Business 360 Approach" to evaluating companies. They not only look at the fundamentals of the companies they invest in, but also at how the companies treat all stakeholders involved— including customers, employees, vendors, and the communities they serve.

This focus on the positive has been an exciting development in the Faith-Based Investing space. While our cultural and political climates become more and more divisive over time, it is energizing to talk to clients about the positive attributes of companies that we invest in—what we can support rather than what we must oppose.

The shift toward positive screening has motivated other companies to follow Eventide's lead. In fact, we created our own "Shining Light Company" blogs where we spotlight one exemplary company each month and share with our followers about these companies. We share how they were founded (many have Christian roots) and how they are striving to make a positive impact through their products and services. We also share how they empower and celebrate their employees and how they bless their communities through charitable giving and engagement with their communities. Clients are encouraged when they hear these positive stories we share with them as part of our review process.

Promoting the positive attributes of the companies we invest in is a compelling approach to many investors, Christian and non. It is also a major factor in shifting Faith-Based Investing to a place of wider acceptance among Christian financial advisors.

Innovation

Earlier we mentioned that one of the obstacles to implementing Faith-Based Investing in an advisor's practice has been the lack of available products to create fully asset-allocated portfolios with the funds that were available. We are happy to report that new product development in the Faith-Based Investing space is at an all-time high!

As more Christian financial advisors learn about and have become convicted about screening their client portfolios, fund companies are listening and creating more screened funds. This is an important development because advisors generally find it very difficult to do the research required to create their own Faith-Based Investing portfolios. While it's still necessary to understand how the different funds implement screening, having access to more funds makes the job easier. The Christian Investment Forum (christianinvestmentforum.org) is a great resource to find a number of the companies providing Faith-Based Investing products for advisors.

Over the last few years, exchange-traded funds (ETFs) have entered the Faith-Based Investing space. This offering has had a major influence in getting advisors to consider screened investing because of the low costs associated with ETFs. There are at least three companies that are now offering screened Faith-Based Investing exchange-traded funds with the anticipation of more to come in the near future.

To overcome the challenges that advisors have with creating their own portfolios, we have created fully asset-allocated, risk-targeted portfolios to give advisors a turn-key Faith-Based Investing solution for their clients. After listening to obstacles that faced independent advisors over the last few years, we became convicted about providing easy-to-implement solutions that would allow the advisors more face-to-face time with clients—the aspect of their job that they love the most. In addition to offering high quality strategic allocation portfolios, we have created tactically managed Core/Satellite portfolios, which had not been seen in the Faith-Based Investing space previously.

In talking with clients over the last two decades, we often found that a majority of a client's assets were held in 401(k) plans. This is especially true of the business owner clients we serve. To create value for these clients, we launched the LightPoint Kingdom(k)â, which is a turn-key 401(k) plan that includes actively managed, fully asset-allocated Faith-Based Investing portfolios in the investment lineup. In addition to filling the traditional roles of plan design, we serve as the fiduciary on the plan, mitigating the fiduciary risk to the plan sponsor and freeing up the advisor to provide ongoing education for the business owner and employees.

Our goal has been to create opportunities for advisors to grow their business without being bogged down by the detailed research required to implement a sound Faith-Based Investing solution. In the near future, we expect to launch a 403(b) solution that will be an excellent option for advisors who serve churches and other faith-based organizations. Be on the lookout for more and more creative offerings in the Faith-Based Investing space as the movement continues to gain traction!

Igniting a Movement

It's encouraging to witness all the positive changes happening in the Faith-Based Investing space. Kingdom Advisors, the premier trade organization for Christian financial professionals, is playing a significant role in this change. Kingdom Advisors has recently expended great effort and resources to help its members develop personal convictions around investing. In addition to biblical principles such as diversification, it is introducing the ideas of investment screening, impact investing, and shareholder advocacy to its members. By providing education and opportunities to discuss the various approaches to investing, it will create opportunities for collaboration and growth to overcome the misunderstandings and division among advisors that existed previously.

The question that has always existed is this: Is there a way to implement Faith-Based Investing in an advisor's practice and still be a prudent fiduciary to clients, or are those objectives mutually exclusive?

We believe these can indeed be complementary goals. When advisors are willing to take time to learn and understand the screening process and to have personal convictions about their goals—what they are and are not willing to invest in— that is the first step to implement Faith-Based Investing in their practice. We think advisors will find that there are many excellent strategies that help round out a client's portfolio.

Interestingly, clients of a Christian financial advisor may assume that their investments are already being screened. We often hear, "My advisor is a Christian, and he would never invest in those kinds of companies." When asked how the advisor introduced the topic of Faith-Based Investing to them, they admit that they have never had that conversation with their advisor. We believe that the time is coming when all Christian financial advisors will be aware of and consider offering Faith-Based Investing solutions to their clients.

It's amazing to witness the speed at which our world changes. Imagine a time in the not-too-distant future where we will be making an out-sized impact in changing the business practices of the companies we invest in. Let's not wait for some undetermined point in the future to align our values with our investments. Let's do everything we can today, in kairos time*, knowing that we are playing our part in making our world better. Won't you join us?

*kairos time - opportune time and/or place--that is, the right or appropriate time

---

References

1. Read more at Fiduciary. (n.d.). in Investopedia. Retrieved from https://www.investopedia.com/terms/f/fiduciary.asp#ixzz5UvXFzxMd
2. Christian Investment Forum. (2017, April). Survey of financial advisors on Faith-Based Investing awareness and use. Retrieved from https://christianinvestmentforum.org/content/uploads/2017/04/Exec-Report-CIF-2016-Survey-of-Financial-Advisors.pdf
3. TIAA-CREF Asset Management. Socially responsible investing: Strong interest, low awareness of investment options; Survey of TIAA-CREF retirement plan participants—2014. Retrieved from https://www.tiaa.org/public/pdf/survey-of-TIAA-CREF-retirement-plan-participants.pdf
4. Christian Investment Forum. (n.d.). "Review of academic studies." Retrieved from https://christianinvestmentforum.org/2017/03/03/academic-studies-performance-esg-investing/

4

THE PERFORMANCE CASE FOR FAITH-BASED INVESTING

BY JASON MYHRE

Many Christian financial advisors rightly picture Faith-Based Investing as a way to please the Lord but wrongly assume that it involves financial sacrifice. As a result, many Christian financial advisors feel they cannot pursue Faith-Based Investing because of the fiduciary duty they have to their clients. This fiduciary duty is seen as seeking the maximum return for invested capital with the minimum amount of risk. Christian advisors may feel pangs of regret in forgoing the opportunity to express their faith in investments, but they feel duty-bound to employ traditional investments to meet their clients' needs.

In sharp contrast with this view, this chapter will argue that applying your faith to investing can be a distinct advantage as a fiduciary, facilitating the task of finding high-performance companies and enabling you to better serve your clients.

Consider a simple illustration. If you had a deep conviction that the world is round, how would it impact you as a National Aeronautics and Space Administration (NASA) engineer? We would all say that this perspective is a tremendous help, right? And you would be at a severe disadvantage if you did not have the perspective that the world is round.

Christianity claims to be nothing less than the true account of reality. If we believe that Christianity is true—and certainly all of us do—then we believe that our faith helps us to see the world in a more accurate way.

Having a clearer set of "goggles" through which to see the world should give us a distinct advantage over our peers who see the world from a very different framework. Ralph Winter, who founded the U.S. Center for World Mission, rightly said, "Every major decision you make will be faulty until you see the whole world as God sees it."[1] This reminder should challenge all of us in all domains of life. For investing in particular, it means that we should seek to invest in those companies whose actions are well-aligned with God's design for the universe. Let's lay out more specifically God's design as it relates to business.

The story of work begins in Creation. In it, God Himself is a worker. He creates the cosmos and everything in it. Everything He makes, He appraises as good; of the whole of His creation, He says, "Very good" (Genesis 1:31).

God creates us "in His own image" (Genesis 1:27). While the full meaning of humanity's God-likeness is hard to fathom, this first chapter of the Bible certainly describes our capacity, like God, for creative and meaningful work—and our ability, like God, to create things that are qualitatively good.

God gives us work. "Then the Lord God took man and put him in the Garden of Eden to cultivate it and keep it" (Genesis

2:15). The last phrase, "to cultivate it and to keep it," is a statement of purpose. Theologians describe this verse as the "creative mandate" or the "cultural mandate"—work is a divine directive. We were made to work. Therefore, work is fundamental to our identity and something that we need in order to live well.

God tells us how to use work. The explanation is found in the words *cultivate* and *keep* in Genesis 2:15. James Davison Hunter, a sociologist at the University of Virginia, writes,

"In the Hebrew derivations, the key verbs are abad and shamar. The former can be translated as work, nurture, sustain, husband; the latter means to safeguard, preserve, care for, and protect. These are active verbs that convey God's intention that human beings both develop and cherish the world in ways that meet human needs and bring glory and honor to Him."[2]

God entrusts us with the task of world-making. In the story of Creation, God planted the garden rich with latent potential but saved the task of completing it for the people He would make. God intends humanity, through work, to be His partner in developing the world. Humanity was to enlarge the locus of the beauty and provision of the garden in all our culture making throughout the world and for the benefit of all.

In the story of Creation, we see that God's design for work itself and all human working, including business, is that it provide for the material needs of the world and bring glory and honor to Him. In this, we see that business, like all human endeavors, is meant to fulfill God's greatest commands to love God and to love our neighbor.

If this is the true design for business, then we should expect that the companies that will prosper best over the long haul are those that best serve the needs of others. And we should expect that investing in businesses that work in harmony with God's design will be the best investment strategy for meeting our clients' needs. And that is exactly what we find.

Let's look at evidences of God's design playing out in business and investing today.

In the book *The Ultimate Question*[3] and in its revised and expanded version *The Ultimate Question 2.0*,[4] leading business management consultant Fred Reichheld sought to identify the single most powerful predictor of business financial success. What he discovered is that companies that perform best over the long term are those that best serve the needs of their customers!

As a result of his research, he said that there is only one question—the ultimate question—that businesses should seek to answer: Are we serving well the needs of our customers? He discovered that businesses that lose sight of this fundamental question are headed for trouble. Listen to his words with ears of faith:

"Too many managers have come to believe that increasing [profits and shareholder value] requires exploiting customer relationships. So they raise prices whenever they can. They cut back on services or product quality to save costs and boost margins. Instead of focusing on innovations to improve value for customers, they channel their creativity into finding new ways of extracting value from customers.

"In short, companies regard the people who buy from them as their adversaries, to be coerced, milked, or manipulated as the situation permits. The Golden Rule—treat others as you would like to be treated—is dismissed as irrelevant in a competitive world of hardball tactics. Customers are simply a means to an end—fuel for the furnace that forges superior profits.

This view is utter nonsense. Companies that let themselves be brainwashed by such a philosophy are headed into the sinkhole of bad profits, where true growth is impossible."[5]

The author developed a metric called the Net Promoter Score (NPS) which measures the degree to which companies create value for their customers. Scoring well on this metric sets companies up for future financial success. To score well, Reichheld says the ethic of service must run deep. He says that in order to achieve a high Net Promoter Score, companies need a second kind of NPS—a Net Promoter System of management. Companies must build service into their operations in a deep and rigorous way.

Further, Reichheld says there is something needed even more deeply still. Companies must have a third NPS—a Net Promoter Spirit animating all their people. Isn't that incredible? Here is a secular business consultant whose research finds that, in order to succeed, businesses must take serving others as the top priority in every way, from management to operations to instilling an ethic of service in all employees. For all the sophistication, the most powerful leading indicator of the future financial success of businesses is the extent to which they serve their customers. Isn't that precisely what God's design for business would lead us to believe? Wouldn't we be smart to evaluate companies the way God does? Absolutely.

In the book *The Good Jobs Strategy*, MIT Operations Management Professor Zeynep Ton sought to understand the relationship between the quality of jobs offered by companies and the financial performance of those companies. Do good jobs make for good performance? Or put differently, do businesses perform better when they meet the needs of their employees? From God's perspective, we should expect the answer to be yes. Work was made to function best when people are afforded the opportunity for meaningful work—where they can engage their creative capabilities and use their unique gifts.

But, how about in low-cost retail—the most cost-competitive segment of the business world? In low-cost retail, profit margins are razor-thin, and it is considered an inviolable truth that bad jobs are a necessary evil for companies to succeed. These companies compete on price. It's assumed that good jobs are a luxury they simply can't afford.

Zeynep Ton chose precisely this low-cost retail world as her parameters for research. She studied closely the companies that offered the lowest prices and enjoyed the highest financial performance in their respective industries, with her research lens focused on jobs. Against the intuition of the world, she discovered that the most financially successful companies were also offering the best jobs.[6]

The key insight from these high-performance businesses was that they all had developed, in her words, "human-centered operations strategies,"[7] a beautiful phrase. Along with important operations management decisions and operational excellence, these companies had put people at the center of their businesses. Rather than viewing people as a labor cost to be minimized, they saw people as an asset to be maximized.

Southwest Airlines, a company at one time well-known for offering the best jobs in the airline industry, was asked why they did it. Herb Kelleher, Cofounder and then-CEO of Southwest Airlines, said, "We take great care of our people; they take great care of our customers; and our customers take great care of our shareholders."[8] When we take care of others, the results take care of themselves.

Here again, we see the wisdom of God's design for business

on display. When businesses choose God's path of serving others, they experience the reciprocal blessing of success. These companies prosper by doing good—and so do their investors.

Let's look at one final study. In The Ultimate Question discussed above, we saw that serving customers was the hallmark of successful companies. But is this success due to customer service alone? Do the products or services themselves matter? The Bain Consulting Group is the organization with which Fred Reichheld, author of *The Ultimate Question*, works. Associates of Bain Consulting wrote the article "The Elements of Value." This analyzed the products and services component of the Net Promoter Score equation. The authors hypothesized that a key driver of high Net Promoter Scores must be coming from the products and services themselves and not only from customer service.[9]

Applying Maslow's hierarchy of needs, they identified four kinds of needs that all people have and organized them into a pyramid of importance: functional needs, emotional needs, life-changing needs, and social-impact needs. Next, they broke down products and services into 30 discrete elements of value across these levels of the pyramid. Finally, they studied how products and services of companies affected performance in two ways. How *many* of the elements of value does the company address? More importantly, how many elements of higher *importance* (higher up the pyramid of needs) are addressed?

Bain found that companies whose products and services met more of these needs and more needs of higher importance had anywhere from three to 20 times the Net Promoter Scores of companies with none. Accordingly, this drove superior profitability and growth.

Ultimately, God's purpose for business is to meet the material needs of the world and to bring glory and honor to Him. When companies channel their creativity into making the goods and services that humanity needs to flourish, they both fulfill this purpose for business and are likely to find success.

There is no conflict between our fiduciary duty and our biblical faith. Our faith is not an impediment to investing for success, but a tremendous resource. As we become even more equipped, more enabled, and more sharpened in our biblical thinking, this will translate into our becoming more skilled investors in the long haul. Rather than being conformed to the thinking of this world, we should seek to transform our thinking by renewing our minds through God's Word (Romans 12:2).

To be sure, we should believe that seeing the world from God's perspective will redound to our benefit. But, importantly, seeing the world this way should also lead us to worship. King David, reflecting on the sacred trust God gave to humanity to rule over the world, wrote Psalm 8 with wonder and adoration of God:

> What is man that you are mindful of him, and the son of man that you care for him?

> Yet you have made him a little lower than the heavenly beings and crowned him with glory and honor.

> You have given him dominion over the works of your hands; you have put all things under his feet.

> O Lord, our Lord, how majestic is your name in all the earth! (Psalm 8:4-6, 9 ESV)

May we, too, be filled with worship as we fulfill our

responsibility of dominion over the world.

References:

1. Ralph Winter. (2009). Perspectives on the world Christian movement: A reader. Pasadena, CA: Institute of International Studies.
2. James Davison Hunter. (2010). To change the world: The irony, tragedy, and possibility of Christianity in the late modern world, (p. 3). New York, NY: Oxford University Press.
3. Fred Reichheld. (2006). The ultimate question: Driving good profits and true growth. Boston, MA: Harvard Business School.
4. Fred Reichheld. (2011) The ultimate question 2.0: How net promoter companies thrive in a customer-driven world. Boston, MA: Harvard Business School Publishing Corporation.
5. Fred Reichheld. (2006). The ultimate question: Driving good profits and true growth. Boston, MA: Harvard Business School.
6. Zeynep Ton. (2014). The good jobs strategy: How the smartest companies invest in employees to lower costs and boost profits. New York, NY: Houghton Mifflin.
7. Ibid.
8. Chuck Lucier. (2004, June 1). Herb Kelleher: The thought leader interview. Strategy+Business. Retrieved from https://www.strategy-business.com/article/04212
9. Eric Almquist, John Senior, and Nicolas Bloch. (September 2016). The elements of value. Harvard Business Review. Retrieved from https://hbr.org/2016/09/the-elements-of-value

5

THE POWER OF SOCIAL SCREENS IN FAITH-BASED INVESTING

BY JEFF ROGERS

The Power of Social Screens to Please...the Owner

The idea behind screening investments goes back to the early days of socially responsible investing when the primary purpose of screening was what we call today "negative screens"—in other words, what *not* to invest in. Typically, these were the so-called "sin stocks" such as tobacco, alcohol, and gambling. Some people, both Christians and non-Christians, have come to see these negative screens as judgmental or legalistic. However, I don't believe that was the intent of the early believers who started to invest according to principles of their faith (Faith-Based Investing), nor do I believe that being judgmental or legalistic is the motivation of most proponents of Faith-Based Investing today. So what is—or what should be—our motivation for Faith-Based Investing? Among the primary motivations are our love for God, our love for others, our desire to be obedient to God's obedient to God's Word, and our desire to be good stewards of the resources God has entrusted to us.

God's Ownership and Our Stewardship

First, we need to recognize that God is the Owner (and Creator) of all wealth.

1 Chronicles 29:11-13 says, "Everything in the heavens and earth is yours, O Lord, and this is your kingdom. We adore you as being in control of everything. Riches and honor come from you alone, and you are the ruler of all mankind; your hand controls power and might, and it is at your discretion that men are made great and given strength."

This is a very rich passage of Scripture with a lot of truths for us to recognize. The truths from this passage include the fact that everything in the heavens and earth is the Lord's. This is His Kingdom—not ours. God is in control of everything, including our businesses, careers, financial opportunities, and the markets. Not only should we adore Him—that is, we should love Him -- but we should also love the fact that He is in control! Finally, riches and honor come from him alone. Read the rest of 1 Chronicles 29:11-13—there's more!

Two of the lies we must come to grips with are the lie of the "American Dream" and the lie of the "self-made man." Because America is indeed the land of opportunity and because we are blessed to have the freedom and the opportunities provided by free enterprise, there are many proverbial rags-to-riches stories. We hear things like the famous quote from Napoleon Hill: "Whatever the mind can conceive and believe, it can achieve."[1] That's a nice-sounding motivational quote, but there is only one problem. It's not biblical! God's Word clearly says that it is God who is in control and that riches and honor come from Him alone.

We hear other nice-sounding things like "pulling yourself up by your bootstraps." Again, those of us who want to cheer people onward to become all that they can be love the thought behind this quote. Unfortunately, though, it also is unbiblical. What does the Bible say about success and the ability to gain wealth? Deuteronomy 8:17-18b says, "You may say in your heart, 'The power and the strength of my hand have made this wealth for me.' But remember that it is the LORD your God who gives you the power to gain wealth." So what part does God play in our ability to create wealth, and what part do we play? Howard Dayton summarized work and wealth this way in his book, *Your Money Counts: "There's God's part, and there's man's part."*[2]

This is true in many areas of life including wealth creation, success in business, and success in marriage and family. What is God's part? He is the Owner, Creator, and Controller of everything. What is man's part? Man is God's steward, His workman and laborer, His servant. Rick Warren emphasizes this truth in one sentence of his best-selling book, The *Purpose Driven Life: "It's not about you!"*[3]

Yes, we must do our part (man's part), and we are to work hard and heartily. We are to invest wisely. But at the end of the day, if God doesn't bless our efforts, we will not have success; we will not create wealth. All of that is at God's discretion and in His control. So rather than think that it's all about us and how smart we are or how great we are, we should work hard "and heartily as unto the Lord" (Colossians 3:23). But then we should ask Him for His blessing, provision, and growth because, without it, we will bear no fruit.

As John 15:5 says, we need to abide in Christ because "apart from me you can do nothing." Think of it this way. The farmer's job is to till the soil, plant the seed, pull the weeds, water, fertilize, and provide the environment for a successful harvest. However, if God doesn't bring the right amount of sunshine and rain, there won't be a good harvest. We share all this to lay a foundation to understand that when it comes to investing—as in all of life—God is the Owner, and we are His stewards. Therefore, how we invest—and how we live all of our lives—ought to please the Owner (God). I like the way my friend Ron Blue puts it: "God owns it all, and I am his money manager."[4] If we begin to see ourselves as God's money managers it will change how we invest His money!

So what does God say about how we invest His money? Many verses (2,350) in the Bible share principles about money, investing, debt, and their impact on eternity, but in 1 Corinthians 10:31 it says, "Whatever you do in word or deed [including investing] do all to the glory of God." So it's really an issue of stewardship. If we truly believe that God owns it all and that we are His stewards, we should ask ourselves the most important investment question: "How can I invest in a way that will please the Owner (God)?"

Negative Social Screens: The Power to Purge

Social screening will, of necessity, include what are called "negative screens." What are the industries, companies, products (including funds and ETFs) that the Owner would not want me investing *His* money in? What are the industries, companies, products, and causes that the Owner would be pleased to have me invest *His* money in? Again, this is not out of legalism or a judgmental attitude. It's because we love God (the Owner). And we love what God loves. And we hate what God hates.

What does God love? People! John 3:16 says, "For God so

loved the world that He gave His one and only Son, that whoever believes in Him shall not perish but have eternal life." Jesus made loving God and loving people the greatest commandments: "Love the Lord your God with all your heart and with all your soul and with all your strength and with all your mind," and "Love your neighbor as yourself" (Luke 10:27). That's it. Love God and love others.

So what does "loving God and loving others" have to do with what we don't invest in (negative screening of investments)? Let me give some examples of things not to invest in because of these principles.

Abortion. Christians believe that life is a sacred gift from God; in fact, God is the Creator of all life. This is the reason we as Christians would *not* want to invest in companies that are involved in or promote abortion. So should we invest in companies, funds, or ETFs that destroy lives that God has created, lives that God considers sacred? There are numerous references to God being the Creator of all life and that He views each life as sacred, but here is just one:

"For you created my inmost being; you knit me together in my mother's womb. I praise you because I am fearfully and wonderfully made; your works are wonderful, I know that full well. My frame was not hidden from you when I was made in the secret place, when I was woven together in the depths of the earth. Your eyes saw my unformed body; all the days ordained for me were written in your book before one of them came to be" (Psalm 139:13-16).

So it is because we love God and we love and hold dear what He holds dear (in this case the lives of all people, including the babies not yet born) that we don't support—or invest in companies that promote or support—abortion. But that's not all. Another reason why we don't want to invest in companies, funds, or ETFs that are involved in abortion is that we love the people involved, the pregnant moms and dads and extended families. We don't want them to experience post-abortion trauma and heartache and regrets like so many who have had an abortion experience. Randy Alcorn in his wonderful books *Why Pro-Life—Caring for the Unborn and their Mothers* and *ProLife Answers to ProChoice Arguments* makes a compelling case, as do many other authors. Some statistics that Randy quotes are that "31% of [women who had chosen abortion] had regrets about their decision." He also said that over 90% said they weren't given enough information to make an informed choice. Over 80% said it was very unlikely they would have aborted if they had not been so strongly encouraged to do so by others, including their abortion counselors. 83% said they would have carried to term if they had received support from boyfriends, families, or other important people in their lives.

And, as Randy says, "Every woman deserves better than abortion."[5]

I couldn't agree with him more. Not only because we care for the yet unborn babies but also because we have hearts of compassion for the women involved and don't want them to suffer the emotional effects and trauma of abortion, we need to ask ourselves questions like this: As God's money managers, would the Owner want me to invest His money in stocks, funds, or ETFs that invest in companies performing or promoting the killing of lives that he considers to be sacred?

Gambling. Like abortion, gambling is another area where, out of our love for God and our fellow human beings, we should consider not investing our (God's) money in companies that conduct or promote gambling. Gambling not only negatively impacts the person with the gambling problem or addiction, it also negatively impacts our culture, our communities, and the families involved. An article titled "Negative Effects of Gambling Addiction" gives some community gambling addiction dangers including increased rates of unemployment, bankruptcy, fraud and check forgery, forced home sales, increased alcohol and drug abuse, and poor mental and physical health of individuals and families.

Gambling is detrimental to that individual and his or her family. Here is what the article goes on to say:

"While the addicted person will definitely suffer during a gambling addiction, that person's family will also face challenges. The stress that the problem gambler experiences may cause irritable behavior, secrecy, and arguments. Calls from creditors and bill collectors erode relationships. Financial strains impact all family members, and strained relationships make the experience difficult for even extended family members, friends, and colleagues."[6]

Children of gambling addicts also suffer in many ways. They may experience:

"Emotional neglect and abandonment (and even physical abandonment) when one parent is consumed in an addiction. Stressed and irritable parents may lash out at children angrily, and even if they do not, these children can sense their parents' tension. Children of people with [a] gambling addiction are at higher risk of experiencing their own addictions later in life."[7]

So applying negative social screens to our investments gives us the power to purge by not investing in things that would displease the Owner and harm those He loves. It's a decision about what *not* to invest in.

As stated before, it is out of hearts of love and compassion for the individuals and families involved that we consider screening out of our (God's) portfolio the stocks of companies that conduct or promote gambling—and the funds and ETFs that invest in them. The same could be said for other activities and industries that make or promote products or services that lead to addiction such as liquor, illegal drugs, and pornography. This also applies to things that create other types of bondage or destroy lives, family, or freedom like human trafficking, sexual exploitation, and all forms of slavery. Our motivation for not investing in these types of companies should not be out of legalism or judgmental attitudes. NO! Our motivation for Faith-Based Investing and applying social screens should be because we love God and we love people—our neighbors, both locally and globally as part of the human race.

There are obviously numerous other things that the Owner would likely not want us to invest His money in. This book is not intended to be prescriptive—telling the readers what to do or not to do, or what companies to invest in or not to invest in. However, we want to share the biblical principles and be willing to ask ourselves the tough questions about how, or if, our faith applies to how we invest our (God's) money.

Romans 14 is a great chapter that outlines the balance of legalism versus Christian liberty, and we would encourage each reader to look at the entire chapter to see how it applies to how we invest on behalf of the owner. Verse 5 ends with "Each one should be *fully convinced* in his own mind" (emphasis added). Most of us have seen the bracelets with WWJD on them which are intended as a reminder for us to ask ourselves, "What Would Jesus Do?" I think that applies to investing as well. WWJII—What Would Jesus Invest In? This includes, what would Jesus *not* invest in—things that violate the principles of His Word or that harm people whom He loves. But it also includes: What *Would* Jesus Invest In? Great question! This brings us to the topic of positive social screening.

Positive Social Screens: The Power to Promote Good

While "negative screening" has been used by investors choosing to invest according to their faith, this area of "positive social screens" is a relatively new and exciting opportunity for us as faith-based investors to apply our faith. Again, this is an opportunity to ask ourselves, "How can I invest in a way that will please the Owner?" I believe the answer lies in investing in the things that God loves— or things that promote the things He loves. What does God love? He loves people, and He loves the family. He loves the "world"—not literally this round ball called Earth, but the people He created on this earth, as we saw earlier from the most famous verse in the Bible: "For God so loved the world that He gave His one and only Son..." So we should show our love for people and consider investing His money in things that help those people—whom He loves.

God loves the family. The family was the first institution created by God back in Genesis. Family is near and dear to the heart of God. Satan, on the other hand, hates God's institution of the family. Unfortunately, there are many companies that are playing into Satan's agenda by intentionally—and sometimes unintentionally—trying to ruin families and destroy even the idea of the traditional, biblical family (one husband and one wife married for life, and children). Many companies, through their advertising—either outright or through what they choose to support with their advertising dollars—are promoting so-called "alternative" lifestyles as well as misunderstood sexual identity, transgender, pre-marital and extra-marital sex, affairs, and pornography. The "alternative" lifestyles used to be called homosexuality and sodomy; but have now been re-defined as gay, lesbian, LGBT, LGBTQ, bi-sexual, etc. (We can clearly see in Romans 1 or Genesis 18-19 how much God hates the sin of sodomy. He destroyed the city by which the sin got its name.)

Satan is (unfortunately) alive and well on Planet Earth, and his agenda of destroying families—and the many lives affected when a family gets destroyed—is remarkably effective. Since, as faith-based investors, we want to invest in ways that bring glory to God and promote what He loves, we should ask ourselves the question, "Would the Owner (God) want me, as His money manager and steward, to invest His money in things that destroy lives and families?" From a positive screening perspective, are there companies that we can invest in that promote God's idea of biblical family units and strengthens families? Yes! Praise the Lord!

A growing number of companies are intentionally trying to produce positive, edifying content that builds people up and strengthens families. For example, we have seen an increasing number of media organizations in movies, TV, book and magazine publishers, social media, and internet-based companies that are trying to be "salt and light" and to present a positive alternative in the area of entertainment. Numerous publishers of books and magazines (both fiction and non-fiction) are intentional in producing content that promotes and strengthens marriages and families. Some of these are publicly traded and easily within the scope of the average investor. Some are private and available only to accredited or qualified investors. Nevertheless, these are examples of how positive social screens can lead an investor to find companies that promote the things that God loves, like the family.

Other areas of investments that affect individuals and families are life, healthcare, and human flourishing. Here again, the use of positive screens is producing some exciting investment opportunities. Eventide Asset Management, LLC, whose motto is "Investing that makes the world rejoice," utilizes a process they call Business 360 which is intended to find companies that create value for all their stakeholders including customers, investors, employees, suppliers, and vendors rather than extract value from them. What a novel idea! And yet, how many publicly traded companies extract value from one or more of their stakeholders out of expediency or an attempt to hit a quarterly earnings target? As Eventide says "Investing can be more than just returns. It's also an opportunity to invest in companies whose products and practices help make the world better."[8]

Examples can be found in the biotech and renewable energy areas. In the area of biotech, advances in technology are developing that could greatly extend the length of life and improve the quality of life of those with certain types of cancer, Alzheimer's, and various rare diseases. In addition, when these advances are successfully developed, they can create value not only for the patients and their families but also for investors and other stakeholders. Win, win, win!

In the area of renewable energy, there are opportunities to improve the quality of life of people throughout the world. For example, pollution now accounts for 16% of all deaths worldwide and has been called the world's largest environmental health risk. In November 2017 *The Washington Post* reported "New Delhi's 'gas chamber' smog is so bad that United Airlines has stopped flying there."[9] Also, air pollution (and water pollution) disproportionately affects the poor of our nation and the world—in places like the West Virginia coal mines; the inner cities of America, China, and India; and other third-world nations. Reducing contaminants and toxins in the air and restricting pollution-causing situations could save millions of lives!

With old and new concepts like bringing hydroelectric power (old technology) to third-world countries where they don't have electricity, we can bring clean power, jobs, water wells, and irrigation to produce more fruitful crops, etc. In addition, with that increased prosperity, we can help them build schools and churches and a new sense of community—a new sense of thriving. As Vernon Brewer, the founder of a ministry called World Help, has said, "We provide help for today and hope for tomorrow."[10]

In the context of new technology, there are tremendous advances in several other areas of renewable energy including high-power and long-life battery cells, solar power, wind power, etc. As these technologies get more advanced and their prices come down, their adoption will increase, and the air pollution will decline! As for the United States, increasing our domestically produced energy (whether through electric-powered vehicles, solar power, wind power, or super-capacity batteries) can reduce our reliance on foreign oil and increase our energy independence. Working through new technology to get old energy out of the ground (fracking technology, for example) can also increase our energy independence. Energy independence is important for our national security as well as our national economy.

This is another example where the right investments in the right companies with the right technology can create value for the consumers, the investors, and even the global community! The global community includes all of God's creatures, and this earth is his creation. From the first man (Adam) back in the Garden of Eden, we were called to be caretakers (stewards) of God's Creation: the animals, the plants, the environment. Let's make the world a better place to live—for all its citizens! Positive social screening can bring about a great difference!

There is another aspect to our stewardship that we need to be aware of—a caution to observe. I must speak the truth in love, and therefore, I must address an issue related to our caring for the environment. Just like Satan twists good things like food into gluttony or sex into iniquity, he also attempts to twist all good things into something evil. One of his primary methods is to get us to love something of God's Creation so much that it becomes something we worship—instead of worshipping God the creator. Romans 1:25 says, "They exchanged the truth about God for a lie, and worshiped and served created things rather than the Creator." This is true in our culture today. The earth and "created things" have become idols that many in our world worship. For example, some people care more about baby seals and spotted owls than about unborn human babies. Others care more about hugging trees than hugging those who disagree with them. (Although they say they are proponents of "tolerance," some of them are the most intolerant.) Still others give more attention to the mountains, oceans, sunrise and sunset (Creation) than they do to get to know the Creator (Artist!) who created them.

So as I advocate for positive social screens that allow us,

as faith-based investors, to invest in things that help God's creatures and take care of His Creation, we need to be careful not to lose sight of who the Owner and Creator is. Our investing—like all of our lives—ought to be an act of worship of our Creator, the Owner, the King of Kings.

The Power to Purify, Redeem, and Transform Communities and Cultures

As followers of Christ we are called to be ambassadors of the King of Kings to the citizens of this world. In doing so, we are to be statesman-like. How would a statesman-like ambassador represent his king to those in a foreign land? He would share the message from his king. He would share this message truthfully, graciously—even lovingly, gently, diplomatically, and winsomely—yet uncompromisingly. That is how we, as Christ's ambassadors to this world should represent the King of Kings! We should not do so out of legalism or with a judgmental attitude. And we certainly should not do so with mean-spiritedness or hearts full of hate. Why? Because we are representing the King with His message, which is, "I love you so much!"

I believe this also affects how we manage the money in our King's treasury (that which He has entrusted to us). Faith-Based Investing, at the end of the day, is investment aligned with our faith, according to the principles of our faith as found in God's Word. This is why some advocates of Faith-Based Investing prefer the term biblically responsible investing. FBI is investing in a way that pleases God (the Owner, our King), and in a way that brings glory to God.

So in closing this chapter, let me ask you to prayerfully reflect on these questions:

How can I invest in a way that will please the Owner?

What would God (the Owner) want me to invest (or not invest) His money in?

WWJII—What Would Jesus Invest In?

References:

1. "Napoleon Hill Quotes," BrainyQuote, accessed April 1, 2019, https://www.brainyquote.com/quotes/napoleon_hill_392258
2. Howard Dayton. (1996) Your Money Counts: The Biblical Guide to Earning, Spending, Saving, Investing, Giving and Getting Out of Debt. Knoxville, TN: Crown Ministries.
3. Rick Warren. (2011). Purpose Driven Life: What on Earth Am I Here For?Grand Rapids: Zondervan.
4. Ron Blue. (2016). God Owns it All: Finding Contentment and Confidence in your Finances. Nashville: LifeWay.
5. Randy Alcorn. (2012). Why Pro-Life? Caring for the Unborn and Their Mothers. Peabody, MA: Hendrickson Publishers.
6. "Negative Effects of Gambling Addiction," The Oaks at La Paloma, accessed April 1, 2019, https://theoakstreatment.com/gambling-addiction/negative-effects-of-gambling-addiction.
7. Ibid.
8. Eventide, accessed April 20, 2019, https://www.eventidefunds.com
9. Wootson, Jr., Cleve R. . and Doshi, Vidhi (2017, November 10). "New Delhi's 'gas chamber' smog is so bad that United Airlines has stopped flying there." Washington Post. www.washingtonpost.com/news/worldviews/wp/2017/11/11/new-delhis-gas-chamber-smog-is-so-bad-that-united-airlines-has-stopped-flying-there/.
10. Vernon Brewer, World Help, accessed April 26, 2019, www.worldhelp.net.

6

THE POWER OF COLLABORATION IN FAITH-BASED INVESTING

BY JOHN SIVERLING

Introduction

As an investor—a Christian investor—you have the opportunity to practice your faith in a unique and impactful way. You can do that by recognizing the difference God can make through you and many others like you in where and how investments are made. The story of the Christian Investment Forum highlights the power we have when we collaborate together as Christians.

In February 2011, a group of Christian financial professionals gathered together in a hotel restaurant to discuss some issues they were all facing in the market. The conversation flowed among those in attendance, with observations and frustrations shared about the slow pace of adoption for an approach to investing known as biblically responsible investing (BRI), also known as Faith-Based Investing. Faith-Based Investing is, broadly speaking, an approach to investing that seeks to invest in and own companies that align with our Christian faith and values. There were differences among those in the room in some of the detailed interpretations of BRI, but the concerns expressed about gaining broader acceptance of Faith-Based Investing were paramount.

Throughout the time together, and in fact part of the very reason for the meeting, was the unifying objective of how to increase the integration of investing and Christian faith. As a result of that meeting, the Christian Investment Forum (CIF) was conceived. From that first meeting to the formation and launch of the Christian Investment Forum the following year, a small group of those from that meeting continued to collaborate through conference calls and working papers to develop the structure and rationale for the Christian Investment Forum that continues to guide us today.

The Christian Investment Forum has a singular purpose: to increase the awareness and use of Faith-Based Investing. This purpose or mission leads CIF and its members to collaboratively engage with financial advisors and Christian investors. As they do, they share the positive story of why investors should care about how their assets are invested, show the impact those decisions can have on our society, and help investors and their advisors understand how they can successfully align investing with their Christian faith. One of the keys for CIF has been to build relationships among its members and with others who share an interest in growing Faith-Based Investing.

The need existed then, and still does, to work collaboratively with others who share a similar interest in increasing the integration of investing with their Christian faith and values. This need exists for several reasons. First, we have the foundation of shared Christian faith, and working together on common goals leads to benefits greater than meeting our own individual needs. Second, collaboration is the best strategy to highlight the positive aspects of Faith-Based Investing and to showcase those aspects to more investors, changing the perspective many have about this growing part of the financial industry. So gaining perspective on collaboration, and how it is relevant to us as Christians and investors, can offer some helpful background.

Collaboration Explained

The term collaboration is very popular in today's dynamic world of business, finance, and management consulting. A quick Google search returned 1.1 billion results for the term "collaboration." The definition of collaboration is, "The process of two or more people or organizations working together to complete a task or achieve a goal."

It's a pretty simple concept, and based on the search results, we are clearly interested in the term. But it is unclear how effective we are in executing the process of collaboration and harnessing the true benefits. That may be due in part to the paradox of collaboration in business. Business, and especially finance, has gained a reputation for being cut-throat and competitive, where only the strongest survive and the winner takes all. Many successful businesspeople have thrived within this framing of business, and some who are unsuccessful in business use that same framing as a reason for their lack of success. As usual, the reality is more nuanced.

The concept of collaboration works against this theme of "us versus them" since it requires sharing and teamwork. Most importantly, it requires some trust and vulnerability to others. Without that, it is inevitable that collaboration will break down when one of those involved focuses on self-interests and decides to forgo the shared goals. Collaboration works best when those collaborating have common vision, values, and goals. They share a mission, so collaborating is logical because it can create strong, mutual benefits.

Collaboration becomes more difficult when our values are less in common. Too often in society and culture we allow differences to become larger barriers than they really should be, leading to arguments or antagonism toward each other. We overemphasize our differences, and they overshadow the goals we have in common. This causes us to lack the ability or interest in cooperating toward a common goal. Collaboration can be challenging when trust and vulnerability move us from our comfort zones. When it gets tough, we often default to our more unchristian state of individualism and self-interest.

Collaboration and Christianity

While self-interest tempts our hearts with the control it offers, collaboration should be at the very soul of Christianity. How else can you love your neighbor if you don't empathize with your neighbor, interact with your neighbor, and support your neighbor and his or her interests? The teachings of Jesus are full of direction for relationships with one another, whether it is a brother or a Samaritan. In Matthew 18:19-20, Jesus says, "Again I say to you, if two of you agree on earth about anything they ask, it will be done for them by my Father in heaven. For where two or three are gathered in my name, there am I among them" (ESV). That seems to be a pretty clear directive to collaborate.

Collaboration is about relationships, and Christianity is essentially a relationship—to God and God's Creation. We are called to oversee God's Creation, even in the current fallen state that followed from our original sin. The only way we can oversee God's Creation is to interact with it, trust each other, and work collectively for our mutual benefit and flourishing.

In his book *Strong and Weak*, Andy Crouch writes about authority and vulnerability when he describes how we can achieve human flourishing. Authority by itself, Crouch suggests, leads to exploitation. Vulnerability without any authority leads to suffering. The result of not having either is withdrawing. It is only by having authority and accepting vulnerability that we can move toward flourishing.[1] The perfect example of this is in the divine person of Jesus Christ, who being God, is omnipotent, but He willingly chose a suffering death on a cross as an offering of saving grace.

Christianity is about working together for a greater good, for flourishing. Arguing for greater good and flourishing should not be interpreted as an argument for or against any specific economic or political theory. Instead, it is about how Christians should act within society regardless of political affiliations (Democrat, Republican, Socialist, Communist, Libertarian), economic system leanings (Free Market Capitalism, Social Capitalism, Socialism, Marxism, Feudalism), or even Christian faith persuasions (Baptist, Catholic, Lutheran, Mennonite, Methodist, Presbyterian, and the list goes on). Christianity should be our primary identity above all else.

Collaboration in Competition

One of the most prevailing false truths spread about work, business, and investing is that they run inherently against the

Christian ethic. Christians and non-Christians alike repeat the mantra that we need to compete in the marketplace "without an arm tied behind our backs" in order to have a chance of success. Others may use this same argument but use it to excuse underperformance because "we had an arm tied behind our backs." In both cases we are reinforcing the idea that it is not possible to succeed in the marketplace unless we use every means possible against our competition, even to the point of violating our moral compass.

Theories like that of Ayn Rand, Milton Friedman and others have been embraced by many in the business community as truth. These theories propose that self-interest and greed are the best means to productivity. They would say that shareholder value maximization means focusing solely on the bottom line of profits no matter the means with which to achieve them so long as they are within the rules of the game. These ideas are not just embraced by those that feel business is inherently corrupt and must be regulated. They are also embraced by those in business who perhaps find freedom for how they act and behave, rationalizing that the ends justify the means. Is there a problem with this kind of theory?

We believe there is a problem. Have we really thought through this idea, or have we allowed others to reinforce it to the point where we accept it without thinking? Is there another way? Is there a better and equally productive way? A growing sentiment that we at the Christian Investment Forum fully embrace is the idea that following biblical principles in our work and investing can lead to maximizing shareholder value and flourishing.

This concept relies on the fact that God designed us for work, and work done with excellence and in accordance with biblical principles leads to productivity and flourishing.

Under this narrative framing, work and investing should rely more on collaboration and relationships with all stakeholders because that is the surest way to ensure value is created for all stakeholders. Substantial research shows that creating value for all stakeholders leads to increased company valuation and true shareholder value maximization.

Even if we believe this narrative, there are plenty of barriers to successfully collaborating in the financial investing market. As already stated, there is an entrenched opinion that the financial industry most especially is not suited for collaboration with its pressure on outperforming the market and the constantly shrinking margins. There are also regulatory concerns that limit what and how much firms will engage in discussion with each other.

More compelling than the problems, however, are the imperatives for collaboration. First, the current amount of investment directed through Faith-Based Investing is tiny in comparison to the overall investment market. Even more significant, the potential market for Christian faith-based investment is 100 times greater than the current market. This large opportunity can only be targeted by providing information to change attitudes and behaviors of advisors and investors. This change can be accomplished by a consistent and clear message delivered through collaboration among individuals and among organizations like the Christian Investment Forum.

Second, the financial and investing marketplace is not a zero- sum market, but instead, one that continues to grow through productivity. With this perspective, the strategy should be less about competing for static market share, and instead, focusing on growing the overall market against the alternatives investors may have. With finite resources available to pursue these gains, it is only through collaboration that progress can be made.

Competing in business and in investing is not about taking from someone else. It is not about winner and losers. It is about being excellent in what we do and about making winners of everyone. Human flourishing is the result of a right-minded view of money and wealth.

Results From Collaboration

The early years of the Christian Investment Forum have demonstrated the importance and value of working together with others to accomplish common goals. These goals are to grow the awareness and knowledge of Faith-Based Investing while still competing with one another. That is only possible because each firm has embraced collaboration with competition. They have accepted that this is not a winner-take-all game with finite boundaries where every dollar gained must be taken from another. They have developed relationships with each other, even friendships with competitors that in the past would have seemed unthinkable. They also compete vigorously, as they should, but always by presenting the positive story of their firm without speaking negatively about their colleagues.

What are the results of this collaboration toward some greater common goal? Christian Investment Forum (CIF) conducted a survey to find out. Between the launch of CIF in 2012 and 2016 there was an 88% increase in advisors who said they were very familiar with Faith-Based Investing. During the same time there was a 73% increase in advisors who felt very well educated on Faith-Based Investing. When asked if they would like to recommend investing that aligns with a client's values, 88% of advisors were very interested. Finally, there was a 48% increase in the number of advisors that were using some forms of Faith-Based Investing with their clients.[2] Much of this progress came from having a common message and presenting that message in a positive way consistently over time. And of great importance, that message didn't attempt to eliminate the nuanced differences in the ways Faith-Based Investing is implemented, so this allows for the continued differentiation of firms and products to meet the needs of investors.

A second result we have seen is the growth in products and firms. A little more than a decade ago there were less than 10 funds or products available to investors interested in Faith-Based Investing. Today, that number exceeds 50 funds, along with many additional options like separately managed accounts, managed portfolios of funds, exchange-traded funds, and others.

There is also a growing list of offerings in the Kingdom-impact investing space for those interested in more direct investments and ownership of companies. This growth is in part due to the recognition of a market opportunity to serve Christian clients well and to offer them products that align with their faith. It is also due to the realization that other advisors and investors hold similar beliefs. That realization brings comfort and confidence to those embracing Faith-Based Investing —that they are not alone in their desire to integrate their work and their faith.

A third benefit of the collaboration between the member firms of CIF has been a growing list of relationships with partners who have overlapping or shared missions. The approach, structure, and messaging of CIF have led to a robust and strategic relationship with Kingdom Advisors, the largest Christian financial advisor network in the country. Other relationships that have been formed and are developing are with organizations such as National Association of Christian Financial Consultants, the Christian Leadership Alliance, Christian Economic Forum, The Lion's Den, The Gathering, and many others. Of course, the very nature of CIF is in building relationships with member firms such as The Signatry. Each of these relationships leads to new opportunities to broaden the awareness of Faith-Based Investing with innovative thinkers and decision makers in the financial industry and in Christian leadership.

Collaboration doesn't mean we agree on all aspects of Faith-Based Investing. There will be differences in approach and in priorities. It does mean we are uniting in some bigger goals despite some of the differences we may have in details. Collaboration shares the bigger vision more broadly and helps everyone see the potential of Faith-Based Investing. And it shows that no one is alone in this desire to integrate faith and investing.

One of the frequent comments I hear is the need to recognize that others are on the same journey. Together we learn from each other; we support one another; we create together; and we build confidence in our mission. This doesn't mean individual firms and funds aren't competing against each other, but they also recognize they are competing against many others with far more distinct values and interests.

Conclusion and the Future

We have seen the power of collaboration at the Christian Investment Forum through the relationships that have been built and the changes that have occurred related to BRI. But that is nowhere near to the full power of collaboration when it comes to Faith-Based Investing. That power will be seen when advisors and investors join with CIF and our members to increase the use of Faith-Based Investing across assets and across the Christian faith.

That power will not just be in terms of the number of assets, but rather on how we view money, wealth, assets, and investing. When that changes, the impact will also be made on people, on relationships, and on our relationships to God. This is the biggest reason for collaboration in Faith-Based Investing and the power it can instill into the other parts of our lives. And its success won't be driven by the Christian Investment Forum or our member firms. It will be determined by you.

What choices do you want to make with your investments? What questions should you ask your financial advisor? If we believe God owns it all, how do we live that out in our decisions about investing? As author and speaker Bob Goff has said, "All the rules change when you're flying under the banner of Jesus Christ. It changes everything, or it changes nothing. It can't just change a couple things."[3]

Regardless of the size of your retirement account, should it be left to the market to decide? Or should it be aligned to God's design for us and help lead us—and others around us—to flourish? Individually the common feeling or response is, "We can't make a difference." But we don't make the difference—God makes the difference through us. And we can make a difference if we trust God at His Word and His promises to us.

Do we efficiently and intelligently use the resources God has granted us to generate returns but also to generate human flourishing? If we believe our wealth and assets are some of our most important resources, are we using them not only as an end to themselves for personal and material wealth but also as a means to a better end?

Ultimately, the power of collaboration in Faith-Based Investing should not, and will not, be measured by simple financial metrics. It should be measured in how we work together, compete civilly, excel in our efforts, love our neighbor, support human flourishing, and live a Christian life that is an example for others.

References:

1. Andy Crouch, *Strong and Weak: Embracing a Life of Love, Risk, and True Flourishing* (Downers Grove, IL: InterVarsity Press, 2016).
2. "2016 Survey of Financial Advisors Summary," Christian Investment Forum, accessed March 28, 2019, https://christianinvestmentforum. org/2017/04/25/2016-survey-of-financial-advisors-summary/.
3. Bob Goff, Kingdom Advisors Annual Conference, (lecture, Orlando, FL, February 19, 2015).

7

THE STEWARDSHIP OF FAITH-BASED INVESTING

BY RACHEL MCDONOUGH

Beginning With the End in Mind

No more tears. No more sadness. No sickness or death. No predators and no prey. No rejection, fear, anger, or greed. The atmosphere of heaven is one of love, joy, and peace forevermore. The Glorious King, who spoke the heavens and the earth into existence and holds the universe together by the power of His Word, has promised that He Himself will wipe every tear from every eye.

I wonder how inspired, encouraged, and motivated we might be if we approached our stewardship journey with that end in sight, rejoicing in the truth that God Himself has already authored our final and most beautiful chapter. His plan for each of us is an eternal life of closeness to Himself, the God of love, and of loving connection with other heavenly citizens, our brothers and sisters in Christ. His plan is a loving family.

At long last, God's children of all colors and languages will be gathered together, perfectly unified by the grace of our Lord Jesus Christ, which is our common salvation and identity. Each one belongs perfectly to all the others, fit together in an intricate, multi-part harmony that is never again disrupted by the discord of envy or selfish ambition.

Yes, to become excellent stewards, we must first see God's ultimate vision for His Creation and for His vast, royal family—beginning with the end in mind.

God Has a Job for You—the Family Business

Having an eternal perspective shapes our earthly role. A *steward*, as you may know, is a trustee or a manager—one tasked with managing resources belonging to someone else. In our case, the Bible tells us that God is the Owner of all wealth (Haggai 2:8). King David stated it in another manner in Psalm 24:1a, "The earth is the Lord's, and everything in it." That means that every asset on every balance sheet legally and irrevocably belongs to Him, regardless of the account title. This is a spiritual reality that supersedes the laws of man.

Despite our lack of ultimate ownership of His financial resources, God, in His grace, gives us meaning and purpose by lovingly incorporating us into His grand design. He allots resources to each of us to manage on His behalf as His stewards. The Parable of the Talents in Matthew 25 implies that God gives an amount to each of us according to our ability.

I like to imagine that His heart and intentions in giving these gifts to us are like those of a parent who gives a set of paints to a child, joyfully anticipating what the child will create. He is, after all, our Father and the Giver of every good gift. He entrusts us with a measure of His financial resources, as well as with other resources: opportunities, time, relationships, abilities, and more. Then He watches and waits with great expectancy to see what we will choose to create with all that He has given to us.

This leads us to the ultimate question of stewardship: What will we do with all the resources He has entrusted to us? He gives us His heavenly wisdom and guidance when we ask for it, but He doesn't control us or micromanage our assignment. He is not afraid of the mistakes we will surely make as we learn how to manage His money. And God, of course, doesn't really need our help at all. He knows no lack that He should be dependent on us to first multiply His wealth so that He might achieve His goals. (In fact, I would guess that God doesn't even have financial goals.)

But rather, as a parent tenderly invites a young child to "help" with tasks around the home or shop, He invites us into the task of managing His resources for our benefit, not His. He uses stewardship tasks to train, equip, and edify us as well as to invite us to connect more deeply with Him. Through stewardship, He simultaneously grows our skills and increases our capacity to think as He thinks and feel as He feels. Our Father uses our stewardship journey as a platform to teach us the family business of bringing heaven to earth.

As It Is in Heaven

When Jesus taught His disciples how to pray, He gave them a specific petition that they could always feel confident in asking of God. It serves as a compass to point them, and us, always and only toward what is true and good. He said we should pray like this: "Let your kingdom come. Let your will be done, on earth as it is in heaven" (Matthew 6:10).

It's easy to get off track when it comes to managing financial resources. Some opportunities look very attractive at first but lead to losses and hardship. It's easy to get caught up in trying to get ahead. At times we might find ourselves rationalizing selfish choices rather than trusting God to supply our needs. But I believe this prayer can help us get back on course as stewards.

Before our time on earth slips away, we would be wise to ask ourselves some tough questions.

Do my financial decisions and habits reflect the values and the culture of heaven?

Has His kingdom, the domain in which He alone is King, expanded into every corner of my personal financial affairs?

Would I hesitate if Jesus walked into my office and asked to take a look at my checkbook register or a list of my stock holdings?

Is there any part of my financial life that is not surrendered to His will?

Do I trust Him alone to be my provider? Or am I making compromises in my obedience in order to increase my net worth?

Am I using His money to build His kingdom or my own?

Matthew 6:10 is essentially our request that God transform this earthly domain into a place that resembles heaven, where His righteous reign is absolutely and completely established. It is the prayer of a wise and trusting child with a surrendered heart—a child who knows that God is a good

Father, and Father indeed knows best.

Said another way, this prayer could be interpreted as, "Father, let the internal atmosphere of my heart and mind, and eventually my external realm of influence in the earth, look increasingly like the Kingdom of Heaven—where Your ways are honored, where love prevails, and where no evil or destructive force is tolerated."

It's a bold prayer. Some Christians might think this world is hopeless to house His kingdom, too corrupt to be made heavenly. But when we are discouraged, we must agree, by faith, with God's Word despite our negative thoughts or feelings. His Word says in Isaiah 9:7 that, "Of the increase of His government and peace, there will be no end."

The way His government (or Kingdom) advances is from inside of us (Luke 17:21); it expands through the surrendered hearts and renewed minds of His children. As we learn and grow through the training ground of stewardship, and through the trials of life, our lives come increasingly into agreement with God and His ways. Upon His mature, faithful, and battle-tested sons and daughters, He confers heavenly authority as His ambassadors.

The Stewardship of Ambassadors

"We are therefore Christ's ambassadors, as though God were making His appeal through us" (2 Corinthians 5:20a). In the same way that the political ambassadors of our day serve as representatives of their home countries while living abroad, we, as followers of Christ, live on the earth as representatives of heaven.

Philippians 3:20 reminds us that our true citizenship is already established in heaven, even while we live out our days on earth. We are here to represent the culture and the values of the Kingdom of Heaven and to be a conduit through which God makes His appeal. The appeal He desires to make through us is essentially the Great Commission—He wants to invite absolutely everyone to be adopted into His family through Christ Jesus.

When our lives are surrendered to King Jesus, we represent the culture of heaven with increasing accuracy. As we mature in the Lord, our lives consistently reflect a culture that contrasts sharply with the world around us. Our resource management choices are a direct reflection of our level of understanding of His ways and His nature.

Radical generosity overcomes old fear- and greed-driven behaviors. Partnership with God grows in our lives where there once was rebellion. Extravagant love for people supplants selfish ambition. A desire for unity disrupts the desire to compete.

As our internal world becomes increasingly heaven-like, our external behaviors also change and stand in contrast to our old ways of navigating life. The impact of this transformation on our stewardship decisions is far-reaching, but I'd like to zero in on how it transforms the investment process.

As an investor of God's money, I can apply an "Ambassador Filter" over every investment opportunity by asking myself these questions:

Am I representing Jesus well as His ambassador if I invest His money in this company?

Does this company somehow reflect the culture and values of heaven (love, joy, and peace)? Dose this company honor, serve, and bless people, as members (or potential members) of God's expansive family?

Is this company stewarding God's money in a way that would please Him?

I believe heaven's storehouses are full of creative solutions for the problems that plague humanity. As an ambassador, it's my job to exhibit the nature of God and the culture of heaven by tapping into God's wisdom and using His resources for the benefit of those around me. If that sounds like an impossible job, that's because it is...if we try to do it alone.

Stewards as Co-laborers

In 2 Corinthians 6:1, Paul uses the Greek verb *sunergeó* to describe this aspect of our relationship with God. It means to work together, to cooperate, or to help in the work. In the NIV Bible, it is translated into the noun "coworker." This relationship is not simply two autonomous persons working simultaneously and side-by-side as we might think of coworkers in a modern corporate setting. Rather, it's all about connection. The only way we can effectively do the work He's called us to is to work very closely with the Boss. In fact, we desperately need to become united with Him in order to succeed.

For me, the biggest challenge of co-laboring with Christ is rightly distinguishing between His responsibilities and my own. It isn't always clear where my job ends and His begins, or vice versa. I think God makes this line intentionally blurry because of His desire for us to depend on Him—something I haven't personally mastered just yet.

I love to work. Sometimes I love it too much. Even though I know that God doesn't actually need my help, I often slip into the mentality that the outcomes are mainly up to me. This leads me to strive in my own strength, rather than work from a position of rest, trusting in his sufficiency and abundance.

In addition, I am at times tempted to define my self-worth in terms of my productivity instead of knowing I'm valuable because of the great price Jesus paid to ransom my life. Thus I am doubly duped into striving, both to prove my value and to avoid having to truly trust God to do His part.

For many years, whenever anyone would ask me how my day was going, I would reply one of two ways. Either I'd say, "Great, I've accomplished a lot," or "Not so good, I've accomplished nothing." Lacking self-awareness, I didn't even realize that I was defining success solely based on my productivity. In short, I've spent over a decade as a willing, and even enthusiastic, slave of my own to-do list.

These patterns of being self-sufficient (not trusting God) and worshipping productivity as my source of worth showed up in my role as a steward. They (along with some healthier motives) have compelled me to work hard at becoming a good manager of wealth.

I created a detailed giving plan. I sampled many budgeting systems before settling on the one I decided was best. I studied the verses in the Bible that related to money, read personal finance books, earned the Certified Financial

Planner™ and Certified Kingdom Advisor® designations, attended financial conferences, executed savvy tax planning strategies, and implemented my estate plan early. I honestly thought that I was doing a pretty good job of managing money God's way until a conference in 2009 made it clear to me that in all of my working I had neglected my heart connection to God.

That was the year I first learned about Faith-Based Investing (FBI). I still remember the uneasy feeling in my stomach when I first came to realize that, as a financial professional, I had been recommending unethical and even immoral investment strategies to every one of my clients. I was so focused on client acquisition and developing efficient business processes that I had never paused to question the moral implications of investing.

In both my personal financial life and in my financial services career, I had been checking things off my lists at full speed without first checking in with Jesus. Despite reading the Bible and having a fairly healthy prayer life, I had kept my faith in its own box, separate from my investing.

I listened uncomfortably as another financial advisor spoke candidly and emotionally about how he had felt compelled to go back to his clients and explain that they were currently invested in businesses that were not in alignment with their Christian faith. He described, with pain and regret in his voice, how he would confess to each client that the reason they were invested immorally was that he, as their advisor, had recommended those investments to them.

When the conference session ended, I went back to my hotel room and wept. My mind was flooded with questions. How could I have been so naïve? Why was I so willing to overlook the moral implications of investing? Why had I never even considered that the profit in my account might be coming from business activities I knew were not pleasing to God?

Many of the Faith-Based Investing concepts were new to me, but I couldn't claim total ignorance. I recalled past discussions about how tobacco and alcohol companies were relatively strong during recessions because people tend to cling to their vices, even when money is tight. I wondered how my heart had been so hard that I didn't mind profiting from addiction. Did I need more money so badly that I would choose to profit at the expense of my fellow image-bearers?

Then there was the issue of abortion. If any issue hits close to home, it's this one. My grandmother was raped in the 1950s. She was not a Christian at that time. Still, she courageously fought to keep the baby that came into her life through that assault, despite being despised and judged as a single mother in that era.

Since she never told anyone what happened to her, she was treated like an immoral outcast, rejected by society and even her own family. Yet she had the righteous determination to protect the unborn life of my mother, no matter what it cost her personally. So how was it that I, only two generations later, could be so indifferent to her legacy that I didn't even bother to ask if some of the profits in my portfolio might be coming from the business of terminating unwanted babies?

The cold, hard truth was extremely uncomfortable. I had been investing God's money in the campaigns of His enemy, businesses that preyed upon human weaknesses and exploited the poor through slave labor. By becoming a shareholder, I had partaken in ill-gotten gain, and worse still, I had encouraged others to do the same. Praise God for His mercy and grace!

In all my stewardship-related activities, with my checklists, tools, education, and Christian resources, I knew I clearly hadn't worked together with God or cooperated with His purposes. In all my researching financial strategies, in all of my striving to be above reproach in paying off debt and giving generously, I had neglected to pay attention to how I was investing God's money. I had never once prayerfully invited God to guide me in my investing, but instead I rushed and pushed forward without Him.

Despite my strong conviction on this issue, it took another four long years before I had successfully integrated biblical wisdom into my practice. Again, praise God for His mercy and grace! Despite my delayed obedience, once I finally did prayerfully invite God into the situation, He graciously began to instruct me in his ways and provided amazing mentors.

At the end of one conference a few years later, I knew it was time to get serious about FBI. I silently prayed for God to send me a mentor, a financial professional who had gone before and had already figured out how to invest with integrity and excellence. I promised Him that if He did that, I would, in turn, help other advisors who wanted to invest this way.

About 30 seconds later, one of the leaders of the FBI movement approached me and asked if I'd like to schedule a series of phone calls to help me get started. He was incredibly generous with his time and information. While I had some nervousness about promoting FBI to clients, I found his courage, and that of other FBI front-runners, to be contagious. Now that my confidence has grown, it is my great joy to invest with a clean conscience and, in turn, humbly share resources, ideas, and strategies with others who wish to do the same.

The fellowship with God Himself and with my brothers and sisters in Christ over this topic has been priceless. Instead of being driven by my old mindset of mistrust, I now feel inspired by the anticipation that I might one day hear the Master say to me, "Well done, good and faithful servant." I want my King to be very pleased with the financial choices I make with His money during my lifetime.

While I do believe that FBI strategies have the potential to result in higher long-term returns, the peace and joy that come from co-laboring with God to bring heaven's atmosphere into earth (in all areas of life) is far more valuable than money. And the closeness to God that we can experience as we co-labor with Him in all things is a foretaste of heaven itself.

8

THE IMPACT OF FAITH-BASED INVESTING

BY MARK REGIER & CHAD HORNING

What Does God Want From Faith-Based Investing?

As we consider how Faith-Based Investing (FBI) can impact the world around us, we may want to start with a few questions.

- What is impact?

- How is FBI impact measured and evaluated?

- And most importantly, what does God want from FBI?

Answering this last question first, we're challenged to reflect on both the vertical and horizontal natures of our faith. The vertical dimension concerns our direct relationship with God—our desire to reflect God's values in our worship, our thoughts, our prayers, and our deeds. The horizontal aspect reflects our relationship with the individuals and communities around us, including our relationship to

Creation itself.

Christ's response to a question about the greatest commandment, recorded in the Gospels of Matthew and Mark, clearly describes these two aspects of faith.

"'The most important one,' answered Jesus, 'is this: "Hear, O Israel: The Lord our God, the Lord is one. Love the Lord your God with all your heart and with all your soul and with all your mind and with all your strength." The second is this: "Love your neighbor as yourself." There is no commandment greater than these'" (Mark 12:29-31, NIV).

Historically, faithfulness on the vertical axis of our relationship to God has been measured through the purity of our choices, actions, and thoughts—often called "holiness." In the field of investing, holiness has often taken the form of avoidance. Like the Quakers avoiding slave-owning businesses in the 1800s or Methodists and Baptists avoiding beer halls and gambling parlors in the 1940s and 50s, religious organizations and individuals have sought to reflect their faithfulness to God's values by the investments they've rejected.

As we move into the third millennium, however, this approach to faithfulness has become more of a challenge. As we address modern slavery found in conflict minerals inside every cellphone and laptop or the sweatshops hidden behind our favorite clothing brands or the racism and sexism that can lurk within even the most respected corporations, being pure is difficult in a complex, interconnected world. In addition, this vertical emphasis focuses on our own reflection of God's purity, overlooking the horizontal call to love our neighbor and other aspects of God's Creation.

How, then, should we live in response to the gift of life and grace from God? What is our response to Scripture with its varied and sometimes confusing exhortations? What does faithful discipleship look like in our time? And for the Christian investor, what does God want from us as we interact with the world through our investments?

What Does the Lord Require?

This question, offered and answered by an Old Testament prophet in Micah 6:8, is fundamental to the concept of Christian discipleship. People of faith are called to "do justice and to love kindness and to walk humbly with your God." Micah tells us that our actions and choices here on earth do matter.

This surprising message follows a series of questions about which offerings and sacrifices are required to bring restoration to the sinning, straying children of Israel. The questions betray a misunderstanding of God's larger purpose, focusing on pursuing the correct ritual for the situation instead of striving for justice and kindness as they interact with others.

Many Christians have taken this call seriously—looking to their faith as a guide for their charitable giving, support for missions, choice of vocation, and the ways they relate to their families and local communities. Far fewer, however, have explored how this call to justice, kindness, and a humble walk with God impacts their investment portfolio.

Learning From the Good Samaritan

If God's values and concerns are the objective of our investing witness, how do we measure and manage the impact our investments are having?

Authentic Christian faith requires engagement in the world, with all its contradictions and nuances. What better example of a person trying to live faithfully in a heated political and religious setting than the Samaritan in Jesus' familiar parable?

What is both ironic and timely is that this parable was offered in response to a question posed to Jesus, asking, "And who is my neighbor?" It is another call focusing on the horizontal axis (relationship with others) of our relationship with God. And it is a question that echoes with importance through the centuries to today.

Found in Luke 10:25-37, this story—in its simplest form—has been baked into American culture. Many, regardless of religious background, will recognize the story of the virtuous man who helped a person in need while others passed by. In short, the Samaritan, from an ethnic group scorned by the dominant culture of Jesus' audience, stopped to help a man wounded by robbers while a priest and a Levite passed him by. These two "holy" men presumably continued on their way because touching the wounded man would have made them unclean, according to the religious rules of the day.

When Jesus flipped a question back to the questioner, asking, "Which of these three ... was a neighbor to the man who fell into the hands of the robbers?" the answer was obvious: "The one who showed him mercy." Jesus emphasized the horizontal relationship between fellow travelers despite their different ethnicities and beliefs and, by doing so, admonished the characters who placed higher value on their narrow understanding of holiness.

We could replace any of these characters with modern

stand-ins and get a similar reflective opportunity. Once again, the call is to action on behalf of the disadvantaged or vulnerable, as opposed to upholding the letter of the law through established rules for holiness and purity—a message repeated frequently throughout the New Testament.

We have just explored a few of the 2,350 references in the Bible to money and resource-related issues, and it becomes clear that the writers and the early church understood the power and importance of the financial aspects of our lives. And while the financial tools of our society differ greatly from those of the first century, many of the challenges remain the same. Several themes emerge from these passages:

- All that we have belongs to God and should be treated as a gift held in trust.

- We are called to be productive in how we use these resources.

- One of God's overwhelming concerns for the use of resources is our impact on the poor, the disadvantaged, and the marginalized.

- Jesus calls us to love our neighbors as ourselves, difficult as that may be.

- The choices we make in the financial parts of our lives are just as important to faithfulness as any others.

Simply put, we are stewards entrusted with caring for and managing God's resources. As stewards, we are challenged to include God's values as we make choices about the use of these resources. We are also responsible to consider the impacts of those choices on others.

The Impact of FBI on the World

Stewardship is an active endeavor, requiring us to navigate the world and all its imperfections. Expressing the concept of stewardship in the markets is messy, but that makes it no less worthy as a framework for the Christian investor.

Many Christian investors start with negative screening. On the surface that approach seems clear cut, but in practice it's impossible to achieve purity when choosing among imperfect companies. While we believe a robust securities-screening framework is a helpful foundation on which to build a portfolio with faithfulness at its core, we will focus in this chapter on other ways to make a positive, faith-oriented impact on the world through investing.

Active Ownership through Shareholder Advocacy

In our financial system, defined rights and responsibilities are conferred to shareholders of public company common stock. If we accept that we are stewards of the gifts God has given us and also accept the responsibilities of being a shareholder, how can we not engage a company when we see injustice?

Shareholder advocacy takes several forms but is most effective when engaged shareholders communicate with company management teams on challenges that, if solved, are in the long-term interests of all shareholders. Unlike protest and boycott, shareholder advocacy happens in private through direct dialogue with corporate managers rather than in the streets and on social media. Shareholders, as owners of the company, have an incentive to see a company succeed while proponents of protest and boycott may not.

Some shareholder advocacy has taken a "guilting" approach, which has worked in certain settings. We believe a more effective approach is to make the case that a change isn't just in the best interests of people and the planet but in the best interest of the company's long-term sustainability.

Most often, faith-motivated investors engage companies on issues related to justice for workers, suppliers, and communities affected by a company's operations. It's rare for shareholders to make a case for change based on biblical truths, as corporate managers are not personally held to this standard by their boards. But faith motivates Christians to advocate for just systems that bring dignity to a corporation and its stakeholders and benefit both in the long run.

Most communication with corporations occurs out of the public eye, often extending for years—during which time trust is built between the parties. If successful, the company adopts all or part of what a shareholder group promoted and may credit itself for the changes, if it believes claiming responsibility serves its interests. Shareholder advocates also may promote the outcome as a success but often must do it in a way that allows the company to accept the credit.

All of this begs the question of whether faith-motivated shareholder advocacy is effective in fostering positive change. Or is it just a way to be a Christian witness in a financial system that operates on a distinctly amoral plane? We believe it has produced and will continue to produce meaningful change.

About 70% of the world's cocoa supply comes from West Africa—primarily Ghana and the Ivory Coast— where hundreds of thousands of cocoa farms operate. It's estimated that tens of thousands of children in this region are employed in the worst forms of child labor in the cocoa- processing industry. These children are often trafficked into the region from poorer neighboring countries, where they may have been kidnapped or sold by relatives to help make ends meet.

These children are unpaid, don't attend school, can't leave the farm, are often physically punished, and perform dangerous work such as handling pesticides and herbicides without safety equipment.

To address this issue, faith-oriented investment firms pursued dialogue with major chocolate companies. Cocoa beans often travel from a farm to a town co-op, to a regional co-op, to a commodity broker, and then to the chocolate companies—the last and most influential links in the supply chain.

Motivated by a belief that we're all children of God and deserve a dignified life with an opportunity to flourish, investors worked with these companies to address child labor in the cocoa industry. They supported government anti-trafficking enforcement, farmer education on child labor, poverty-reduction programs, improved agricultural methods, and programs to help farmers become certified growers.

Due in part to years-long dialogue, The Hershey Company committed to sourcing 100% certified cocoa immediately for its Bliss line of chocolates, then followed up a few years later by committing to source 100% certified cocoa for all its chocolate by 2020. This successful shareholder advocacy effort, emphasizing caring for one's neighbor (in this case child workers in West Africa) ensures that more cocoa is farmed using standards to protect the environment, employees, and communities without the use of forced and child labor.

Other examples of shareholder advocacy led by Christian institutional investors include addressing labor abuses associated with mineral mining in areas of military conflict and the exploitation of workers at the margins in corporate supply chains—particularly in the food industry.

The Bible implores us to care for widows and orphans and argues for fair treatment of slaves. Of course, our society prohibits slavery in the form practiced in the days of the Bible, but forced laborers working at the lowest rungs of the corporate system and with very little control over their working conditions are today's slaves.

Active Proxy Voting Moves Management to Respond

Because most shareholder advocacy occurs in the background, many investors only see its effect in the form of shareholder-initiated resolutions on corporate proxy ballots. Shareholder advocates typically resort to resolutions only when companies are unresponsive to offers for a conversation or when dialogue results in an impasse.

The Securities and Exchange Commission must approve shareholder-initiated corporate resolutions before they're allowed on a ballot. When enough shareholders vote in favor of a resolution, corporate managers usually take notice and address the concern, even if the outcome the resolution requests isn't mandatory.

In 2018 shareholders filed hundreds of resolutions addressing environmental and social concerns with U.S. corporations, but many were withdrawn before going to a shareholder vote because the companies were willing to discuss the issues. Proxy voting campaigns have focused on the risks of climate change as well as forced labor and human trafficking in corporate supply chains.

Mainstream investment firms recently have supported shareholder resolutions in larger numbers. In the case of climate change proposals, the median proposal was supported by over 30% of shareholders in 2018, signaling support from many large traditional investment firms.

Whether motivated by faith, altruism, or profit, investors are joining shareholder advocates in communicating clearly with company management teams who must respond or face continued pressure.

Channeling Investment Dollars for Positive Impact

Another powerful way for Christians to extend their impact on the world is to direct investments in support of life-affirming enterprises and projects. Over the last decade, the global fixed income market has developed positive impact bonds, including what have become known as "green bonds." Green bonds have a specific, positive environmental objective in addition to the market rate financial return expected of this type of security. Other impact bonds support affordable housing, human-development objectives, and health outcomes, to name a few.

The Earth Is the Lord's and All That Is in It

This familiar opening line from David's song in Psalm 24 reminds us that God is the Founder of all that exists – earth, sky, and sea—and the people who reside here. This simple, yet awesome, statement reinforces God's undisputed ownership of the universe and sets up humans' roles as stewards of God's earthly resources in other passages. If we are stewards, we are responsible for the earth and its fullness.

Electric utility companies are increasingly issuing fixed-income securities that fund sustainable energy projects. These alternative sources of energy are supplementing the baseload capacity of American utilities that mainly generate electricity from burning coal and natural gas. By exploring new ways to power our lives, we extend the resources God entrusted to us.

Positive impact bonds can also address the injustice of the uneven opportunities that God's people experience around the globe. In 2004 the governments of the United Kingdom and France launched a proposal for immunizing millions of children in Africa. The International Finance Facility for Immunization (IFFIm) was formed and joined by other Western countries, and a market rate bond was issued. As a direct result, millions of children around the world received life-saving immunizations sooner than they otherwise would have because of this innovative way of using financial markets to solve a human-development challenge.

In the Americas, the Inter-American Development Bank (IADB) has issued an Education, Youth, and Employment (EYE) Bond designed to support loans that focus on education, youth, and employment programs in the Caribbean and Latin America. IADB is a multifaceted financial institution whose projects promote sustainable growth, poverty reduction, and social equity programs in that same region. It is also committed to bringing about development in a sustainable, climate-friendly way. Through investments like this, Christians can supplement the mission, relief, and development activities of their favorite ministries operating in these same regions and communities.

Community Development Investing

We believe Christian investors have ample ways to bend the arc of history in the direction of justice through market rate investments. But there is also a place in portfolios for extending capital to organizations that provide economic opportunity for disadvantaged individuals and communities. These community development organizations serve populations on the margins of society with affordable housing, job training, microfinance, and economic development.

Typically designed as fixed-income instruments, these investments often pay interest rates lower than market rates in a concession to the mission of the institution and its clients. This type of investment combines investing and giving in a single package, employing the means of the financial system in service of the ends of a worthy mission.

One example of this type of investing is through vehicles like Calvert Investment Notes and their support of Benefit Chicago, a MacArthur Foundation initiative to enhance job readiness, create jobs, and build wealth in underserved communities.

One of the organizations receiving capital through this program is Sweet Beginnings. Sweet Beginnings offers a honey-based product line while providing job training opportunities to community residents who, due to former incarceration or other circumstances, have a tough time getting hired. Sweet Beginnings' clients are just trying to get a break in a society that is wary of their past, not unlike the neighbors the Bible implores us to help.

Reflecting God, Impacting Others

The impact of FBI in the world lies both in our relationship with God and with others. Striving for holiness in our entire being—our thoughts, intentions, and worship—provides a spiritual foundation for working on behalf of our neighbor. It is through our active, impactful, daily activities that we demonstrate love for our neighbor.

Fortunately, our modern financial system affords Christians numerous ways to live out God's call to be stewards of the resources of the universe and to do it in ways that show care and, therefore, impact our neighbors.

Whether through advocating on behalf of the voiceless, communicating to corporate management teams through proxy votes, or directing investment dollars toward positive activities, we have the call and the opportunity to do justice, to love kindness, and to walk humbly with our God.

9

MAKING A GRACE-FILLED CASE FOR BIBLICALLY RESPONSIBLE INVESTING

BY DWIGHT SHORT

When I decided to incorporate biblically responsible investing (BRI) into my practice with clients at Merrill Lynch, I was convicted about the process. I would need to do this in my own investing habits and processes first, before asking my clients to consider it. I had a significant following from Jewish families. My respect for them led me to evaluate whether I should ask them to consider the Bible that I read—including both the Old and New Testaments—as a source for investing decisions. Or is it morally right to ask them to focus only on Old Testament instruction?

Some advisors have felt the calling of God to stop working with clients who do not follow along with BRI principles. These advisors believe that it is unlikely that they can do good work for anyone when following different philosophies. There may be merit to such a position, and I respect it. But in my own walk, I have never led anyone to Christ by starting with a point of view like, "This is the way I live my life, so I expect you to do the same." When I started sharing BRI, it was similar to my witness in general. I have decided to invest this way because my motivations as a Christian cause me to live and to invest in a way that is different. It is also motivated by my desire to serve my Savior as the best steward possible of the assets and responsibilities I have been given.

This is living by the grace of God, a grace that I extended to all who would listen to my passion about investing as an act of worship. This grace-based principle found a myriad of reactions. Almost every Christian believer with whom I discussed BRI wondered what the cost would be. It seemed like an effort to bargain with God as to whether this potential sacrifice of time and performance would have to be resolved only by divine intervention. How could someone ever hope to determine which companies were good enough to make it into an acceptable BRI portfolio? Suppose serving the Lord means that you will earn two percentage points less on your investments. Would this make you choose not to invest by biblically responsible investing principles? What if you earned 5% less? Do we start bargaining with God to see if we want to be obedient?

This too allows some people to dismiss BRI as something that is too idealistic and too impossible to achieve, so why try? My challenge to those who feel that way is that they do not live the rest of their lives in similar denial. We are humans; we are sinners; we all have weaknesses. So what good is it to try to make moral decisions? Since it is too hard, why try?

As parents, we do not let our teenagers off so easily. We don't allow them to take any and all actions in life any more than we should allow our portfolios to be invested without a moral or biblical compass.

When we invest in companies that cause addictive behavior, cause obvious harm to the environment, perpetuate sinful activities, produce and/or transmit pornography, or profit from other activities we know to be sinful, we are pretending our investing decisions do not make a difference. Because these investments are usually done in a passive way, the leaders of the companies we own do not usually know of our angst about what they might be doing. The leaders of the companies may not know or care, but in our own heart of hearts, we know!

While my Christian clients counted the cost before agreeing to make changes in their investments, I was shocked by the acceptance of my Jewish clients to being part of any process that improved moral and ethical standards. So grace begins with our ability to allow others the time and space to process the ideals of biblically responsible investing. But grace never allows us to dodge our responsibility by pretending that a problem doesn't exist.

Many sincere Christians believe that the effort to accomplish BRI is beyond their scope of influence and that to make the effort is a waste of time. They have listened to the idea and find it credible and interesting, but the implementation is so complicated, in their opinion, that they have dismissed it out of hand. Earlier we discussed the appropriateness of making moral judgments in investments. This question is similar: Should we use whatever influence we have to promote faith-based investment practices? The foundational question of both debates is the same. How can a serious Christian knowingly profit from investments in activities that he or she knows to be sinful?

What often happens in the name of grace, or just in the name of being peacemakers, is that the biblically responsible investing advocate will look upon those who have not adopted BRI as ones in need of prayer and of more time to come around to the truth. That truth is built on the premise that all we do and that all we invest in does impact our walk, our worship, and, of course, our stewardship. So there are investors who have adopted BRI practices and await the work of the Holy Spirit in the lives, hearts, and portfolios of all believers to join the ranks.

A most valid criticism for adopting biblically responsible investing centers on the widely accepted practice of portfolio diversification. The range of choices for BRI providers when trying to diversify across all the appropriate asset classes can still be limited. International providers are still among the hardest to find, while even real estate investment trusts (REITs) can be problematic. Larger investors who are committed to finding a way to accomplish their biblically responsible investing goals have invented their own exchange-traded funds (ETFs) for meeting these goals, but for the average investor, these options are not so easily found. Those that have come onto the market are often so small and illiquid that advisors are reluctant to use them for their clients. Over time, this is likely to change for the better, and we see several organizations that have plans to launch ETFs to meet the goals of BRI investors. This will also remove one more barrier and allow more people to invest according to their moral persuasion.

In my book *Kingdom Gains*, I highlight for investors, advisors, and pastors what their decision-making models might include as they consider the merits of BRI. As a thought provoker in this process, I added a few quotes from Christian leaders and theologians who offered insights that hit clearly on the subject. The following is a quote used with permission from author and lecturer Ken Boa:

"We have seen that holistic spirituality involves a growing responsiveness to the Lordship of Christ in every internal and external facet of our lives. It is not a question of developing a list of theoretical priorities (e.g. God first, family second, work and ministry third, etc.), but more a matter of allowing the centrality of Christ to determine and empower what we should do in each day. Seen this way, Christ is our Life and Lord in all our activities, and whatever we are doing at the moment becomes our priority focus. When the grace of Christ rules in our lives, we will better discern how to allocate the resources God has entrusted to us."[1]

In all grace, I challenge you to lay all of yourself on the altar and ask God to examine your life, your work, and all your actions, including investment activities. It is not someone else who benefits if you invest just like every other individual, nor does someone else benefit if you are prompted to invest with a Christian moral compass. It is your life that will change! It is your relationship that will grow in a different way! Indeed, it is you who will come closer to the Lord as you seek His will in one more aspect of your life. Blessing to you on this wonderful journey!

The next step we recommend is to visit a portion of Scripture that was first shared with me relative to biblically responsible investing by Ronald Blue. Ron has been an important encourager for many of us who felt called to offer insights through the written word, but his challenge to me was that Romans 13 and 14 have much to say to those who have not yet accepted BRI. It seems clear enough that any activity that a Christian participates in expresses an endorsement.

However, in this part of Romans the Apostle Paul suggests that not all these things carry the same level of priority. We need to allow people the time to consider and study activities such as BRI so that each person may be convicted in his or her own way. God does want to work through you in a unique and specific way so that your witness is most effective.

Plenty of admonition comes to us in Romans 13 and 14, where Paul refers to those who are stronger in their faith to be understanding of those who are weaker. In this case, if you have already decided biblically responsible investing is an important part of how you will invest, then you should advise and set an example. Others may need to process that same idea for themselves before taking such a position. Does it mean that in not practicing BRI they are in fact committing sinful acts? Only God can determine sin in one's life, and conviction will never come from a friend or colleague alone without the Holy Spirit providing the tug on one's heart to make a change.

These verses may serve as a starting place for your decision-making:

"But put on the Lord Jesus Christ, and make no provision for the flesh, to gratify its desires" (Romans 13:14, RSV).

"We who are strong ought to bear with the failings of the weak, and not to please ourselves; let each of us please his neighbor for his good to edify him" (Romans 15:1-2).

"Who are you to pass judgment on the servant of another? It is before his own master that he stands or falls. And he will be upheld, for the Master is able to make him stand. One man esteems one day as better than another, while another man esteems all days alike" (Romans 14:4-5).

Even the Apostle Paul, who was one of the most direct and courageous believers, doesn't advocate an in-your-face approach. As you either present the case for biblically responsible investing or consider the case for BRI, allow your heart and your head to work in concert to ponder the merits. Will your Christian walk be enhanced by this effort? Will it result in your having more chances to share the Gospel as people find out that you have changed how you invest? If you are an advisor and are worried about how this might affect your relationships with clients, it is important to know how you will understand BRI for yourself before you start asking others to join in.

You are unlikely to be successful in presenting biblically responsible investing to anyone if you haven't decided to put it into practice first. This is a case of not being able to lead someone where you have never gone in the first place. When I decided to take this approach into my practice at Merrill Lynch, we had no resources to support biblically responsible investing. In good conscience I could not demand everyone do this when it was so new to me and so untried. So my pitch was not "either you do this or else." I simply let people know that I was beginning to do this personally and here are the reasons. "I want you to know, Mr. or Mrs. Client, this is what I feel called to do in my own life, and I want you to consider whether you would like to go with me on this journey."

Many did; many more did not! I was blown away by the large number of clients who did want to join me in the journey of biblically responsible investing. I recommend that you and all those whom you influence do the same. A final word of admonition:

"I appeal to you therefore, brethren, by the mercies of God, to present your bodies [and your portfolios] as a living sacrifice, holy and acceptable to God, which is your [reasonable] spiritual worship. Do not be conformed to this world, but be transformed by the renewal of your mind, that you may prove what is the will of God, what is good and acceptable and perfect" (Romans 12: 1-2).

References:

1. Kenneth Boa, *Conformed to His Image: Biblical and Practical Approaches to Spiritual Formation*. Grand Rapids: Zondervan, 2001, p. 243.

10

IMPLEMENTING FAITH-BASED INVESTING IN YOUR PRACTICE

BY LORAN F. GRAHAM

"I am confident of this, that the one who began a good work among you will bring it to completion by the day of Jesus Christ" (Philippians 1:6, NRSV).

If you are a financial advisor considering Faith-Based Investing for your practice, this chapter is for you. As a trusted advisor, you are uniquely positioned for influence. Money is a tool that touches nearly every aspect of life. It can also be a test and, ultimately, a testimony of our values. We have the privilege and responsibility to speak truth into the lives of our clients and share biblical principles to help guide them on their financial journey.

Are you excited about the idea of honoring God with investment choices? Do you think your clients could get excited too? If the answer to those questions is yes, keep reading. You may be ready to jump in with both feet and convert your entire practice to Faith-Based Investing. Or perhaps you are simply testing the waters and considering sharing this approach with a few of your clients. That is okay!

Wherever you are in the process, the decision to implement Faith-Based Investing in your practice may feel like you are standing on the edge of a cliff, looking out over a great unknown. What will my clients think? Will I lose clients? Will my practice suffer? Is there enough demand in my community to sustain a Faith-Based Investing practice? These fears are normal. At least, that is how I felt with my own practice when I stood at this precipice nearly a decade ago. As I share what I have learned on my own professional journey, my hope is that this chapter will provide some practical wisdom to help you get started.

My introduction to Faith-Based Investing came in 2009 at a biblically responsible investing seminar in Seattle. I walked away with many questions, but a seed was planted in my mind. Nearly a year later, I was still wrestling with the question of whether or not to introduce this approach in my practice. I needed to conduct more due diligence. In 2010 I traveled 2,400 miles from Washington State to attend a Kingdom Advisors conference in Atlanta. At the conference I met with several investment managers and national leaders who were early pioneers in the field of Faith-Based Investing—many of whom authored other chapters in this book! At the end of the conference I remember placing a call to my best friend, a former hedge fund manager and successful entrepreneur, and exclaiming, "I think I have found my calling!"

A Leap of Faith

Returning home, I floated the idea of following my passion and converting to a Faith-Based Investing practice. I talked to a couple of financial advisors who were mentoring me at the time. I was told that it would not be a smart business decision because there was not enough demand. They said that I would never find enough clients to be sustainable and that the clients would not find me. It was scary to receive that kind of advice, and yet I felt the tug of God on my heart. Has God ever called you to take a step of faith into uncertainty or danger? I can only imagine what Moses must have felt when God commanded him to lead His people against the most powerful nation on earth. Much like Egypt, which was the center of civilization at the time, Wall Street's influence on our capital markets—and on our culture—is far-reaching. I have often heard Ron Blue say, "If you change Wall Street, you change the world." I am certainly not comparing myself to Moses, but I can relate to the time he pleaded with the Lord:

"'Pardon your servant, Lord. I have never been eloquent, neither in the past nor since you have spoken to your servant. I am slow of speech and tongue.' The Lord said to him, 'Who gave human beings their mouths? Who makes them deaf or mute? Who gives them sight or makes them blind? Is it not I, the Lord? Now go; I will help you speak and will teach you what to say'" (Exodus 4:10, NIV).

I believe that sometimes God calls us into seemingly impossible situations in order to demonstrate His power. It is a divine mystery to me that God uses imperfect people to accomplish His perfect purpose. Over a decade later, I have been humbled to see how the Lord has provided, and today we have a thriving Faith-Based Investing practice.

The Case for a Faith-Based Investing Practice

It is one thing to be passionate about a certain subject matter. However, as a business owner and entrepreneur, I understood it must also make financial sense. After all, being responsible is an important component of good stewardship. I believe that responsibility is where many advisors wrestle. In my practice, two books were influential in helping me make the leap from being passionate about the concept of Faith-Based Investing to believing that it could be a sustainable business model. Interestingly, these books were not Christian books. Both are business leadership books ranked high on the best-seller lists, and together, they gave me a compelling vision for developing a faith-based professional practice.

The first book that influenced me was *Start with Why: How Great Leaders Inspire Everyone to Take Action* by Simon Sinek. In that book Sinek argues that the key to success for organizations is understanding why they exist.[1] Why did you start a practice? What do you believe? Sinek's book helped me realize early on that I could not be all things to all people. I needed to clearly define our organization in terms of a compelling vision and mission statement.

For me, the vision was to inspire our clients to think about how they may honor God in every area of life, not just financial decisions. If you haven't developed a vision and mission statement for your practice, or if you feel it is in serious need of updating, I highly recommend you start there. Carve out a full-day retreat with your staff somewhere offsite and design vision and mission statements for your practice. Explore how Faith-Based Investing may fit into that equation. There are countless business leadership resources that can guide you in the process of developing a vision and mission, so I will not go into that any further here. But this process was an important milestone for me in moving toward a Faith-Based Investing practice.

When I considered our identity as an organization, I was able to articulate a key differentiator. All my professional advice flows from a biblical worldview, based on Psalm 24:1-2 and other Scriptures. I believe God owns it all, and we are just stewards, or managers, of whatever resources are entrusted to us. That's what we teach our clients. Over time, I have come to learn that this applies not only to money and passive investments but also to my business entity. Sure, the title on the door may read, "CEO/President," but God is the Chairman of the Board and Sole Shareholder. Ultimately, I am accountable to Him for how I have used His resources to further the work of the Kingdom and bless those we serve. "The earth is the LORD's and all that is in it, the world, and those who live in it; for He has founded it on the seas and established it on the rivers" (Psalm 24:1-2, NRSV).

The second book that influenced me was Jim Collin's book, *From Good to Great*. In that book Collins outlines what separates truly great companies from mediocre ones. That really got my attention. Collins shares a wealth of information for entrepreneurs, but the concept that impacted me most was what Collins described as "The Hedgehog Concept."[2] According to this concept, great companies ask three very important questions:

The first question is, "What are you most passionate about?" As I shared earlier, Faith-Based Investing is high on the list. What gets you excited to wake up in the morning? Clients can sense where your passions are. Passion can also be contagious, and your clients will assign importance to the things that you believe and communicate are important.

The second question is, "What drives your economic engine?" Cash flow is the lifeblood of any business. Without revenue, a business is no more than a hobby. There are many compensation models for financial advisors, but for the most part advisors charge fees for the investment advice that they give. In my practice, advisory fees for portfolio management represent over 95% of our annual revenue. If our advisory fee income were to evaporate, so would the practice! As a matter of professional ethics, we always put our clients' best interests above our own. Accordingly, the decision to implement a Faith-Based Investing practice was not something that I took lightly. It is mission-critical that we get this right for our clients.

The third question was what really got me, "What can we be the best in the world at?" According to FINRA, there are over 630,000 registered advisors in the United States.[3] Needless to say, it is a highly saturated and competitive industry. What sets you apart in the marketplace? The wire houses, banks, and big-name Wall Street firms spend millions of dollars every year on advertising to explain to investors why their solution is best. Ironically, in an era of intense competition, many firms struggle to set themselves apart. The fact is that asset allocation and risk management strategies are starting to look more and more alike from firm to firm as industry best practices become standard practices. Can you really diversify better than the wire house firms and global firms managing trillions of dollars? Perhaps. Is there an area of the marketplace that is underserved at which you can be the best in the world? Perhaps! Faith-Based Investing is a niche market that is underserved and where there is great demand.

Imagine these three questions in a Venn diagram (three overlapping circles). Where they come together in the center is what creates the most opportunity for you to stand apart from the rest as a financial advisor in a highly competitive industry. Faith-Based Investing presents an exciting opportunity for advisors willing to take a step of faith to meet this growing demand.

"Then he said to his disciples, 'The harvest is plentiful, but the laborers are few; therefore, ask the Lord of the harvest to send out laborers into His harvest'" (Matthew 9:37-38, NRSV).

I have made a case for why it may make business sense to implement a faith-based practice. The next step is to make sure your firm will provide the support you need to move forward.

Equally Yoked

Is your RIA firm or broker and dealer onboard with Faith-Based Investing and biblically based financial planning? Are other advisors in the firm free to operate a faith-based practice? Will the firm be agreeable to Faith-Based Investing content on your website? These are important considerations. What about their trading platform? Will the firm provide access to a broad selection of faith-based solutions from which to choose? Do they have the scale and infrastructure to provide adequate technology to implement it? This includes providing an efficient trading platform at a reasonable cost. If you are utilizing third-party managers to implement Faith-Based Investing models, what is their due diligence process? In everything that we do, we seek to serve with excellence. This includes having quality business relationships and vendors in place to support a faith-based practice. "Whatever your task, put yourselves into it, as done for the Lord and not for your masters, since you know that from the Lord you will receive the inheritance as your reward; you serve the Lord Christ" (Colossians 3:23-24).

A Menu of Confusion

Assuming you have the right business relationships in place to launch your Faith-Based Investing practice, what does it actually look like to operate one? Before I clarified my mission and vision, I started to introduce Faith-Based Investing to clients as a menu of choices. Clients were invited to consider this new Faith-Based Investing methodology—which I was passionate about—or they could continue utilizing traditional fund managers who were "values-neutral." I chose that terminology because traditional investing methodologies do not seek out unbiblical companies. The moral issues are simply not on their investment research radar. I presented both proposals with performance history and graphs and explained the risks. I explained that the Faith-Based Investing selections introduce an additional layer of research, evaluating the investment opportunities for moral considerations. About 60% of my clients went for it. To cover all my bases, I even offered a middle ground, "socially responsible investing" option, which was mostly environmentally focused. There were some clients who gravitated toward that as well.

Suddenly, I was faced with a new challenge. I found myself managing three sets of third-party manager platforms and basically trying to be all things to all people. A couple years later, after much prayer and deliberation, I decided we were going to be a Faith-Based Investing firm. We would be inclusive to any client who was comfortable with our biblically based investing approach, but we could no longer be all things to all people. For the 40% of clients who were not yet onboard, I took a step of faith and had "the talk." I explained that we were focusing all our energy and investment research in one area—Faith-Based Investing—where we think we can be "the best in the world," and we hoped they would come along. To my surprise, we had nearly 100% retention of client relationships in that process! Not everyone shared the same moral views on all the faith-based screens, but they trusted me and were willing to come along. That was huge for me. Praise God!

It was also an important lesson. The client families we work with hired me for one very important reason. They trusted me. They trusted in my professional competence. They trusted that I will always do the right thing and put their best interests above my own. In a world of constant headlines about financial corruption and fraud, make no mistake about it: Trust is the number one reason your clients are with you. They trust you! I truly believed, and still believe, that by concentrating my efforts in this one specialty area, I would better serve my clients than trying to be all things to all people. I was choosing to be a specialist, instead of a generalist. Our clients understood and appreciated our motivation—that we were making these changes in an effort to better serve them.

Achieving Clarity

Once we made that change, another interesting thing happened. My batting average for onboarding new client relationships went from about 50% to over 80%. We were winning more business! Why? Prospective clients meet with us because they are looking for clarity. They are bombarded with choices and options and are looking for a trusted advisor to give sound recommendations and guide them on what to do. By presenting a "menu" of choices, it was actually throwing up a roadblock in the prospective client's mind. We were asking them to choose to trust us as an advisor and choose a methodology (values-neutral or Faith-Based Investing) in the same meeting. As a result, we ran the risk of paralyzing the potential client in indecision. They are sitting there in the meeting thinking, "I've never heard of Faith-Based Investing, and you are asking me to choose!" Once we defined who we are and what we offer, I developed more confidence. They could sense my passion, and I was no longer asking them to make multiple choices simultaneously.

Now, we are crystal clear on who we are and the service we provide. In every initial consultation meeting, we simply explain that service as part of our value proposition in the stewarding of wealth for our clients. We aim for the best returns for each client's individual needs, risk tolerance, and objectives, while at the same time aiming to make a positive impact in the world through Faith-Based Investing. And we invest this way for everybody! I then will ask, "Does that sound like the type of firm you are looking for to help you manage this wealth you've been entrusted with?" To our surprise, often we get an overwhelming, "Yes!" Or our value proposition will catch the prospective client's curiosity just enough to ask questions. "Tell me more." That is still a great response! So we continue. "Well, we work with investment managers who are looking for great investment opportunities, because after all, the purpose of investing is to seek returns! We are simply adding an additional layer of research, to test whether that company's product or service is compatible with biblical values. Does the product cause physical harm to others? Does it prey on the weaknesses and addictions of others? If so, the fund managers go back to the drawing board." I explain that, as a result, we will invest in certain industries and not in others, and we gravitate toward companies whose products and services lift up humanity and reflect biblical values. Of course, we are careful to explain some important disclosures: that past performance is not a guarantee of future results, that all investing involves risk, and that no diversification strategy ensures against loss. I even go a step further and point out that for social, moral, and faith-based investments, returns may be lower than if the investor made decisions based solely on other investment considerations, but they could also be higher. While there is a lot of data out there suggesting that social and moral screening does not necessarily hinder performance, we do not want greed to be the motivation.

Interestingly, we found that this approach was attractive to not only Christian clients, but also clients of other faith traditions and philosophies who share our moral values. For us, that is great! We want an inclusive, diverse practice. But the common thread that makes us a client community is the investing approach—everyone invests in our Faith-Based Investing models. Remember, Faith-Based Investing may be intriguing to the client, but the number one reason that prospective client is sitting at the table in your office is because he or she trusts you. We have found over and over again that trust is what clients value most in the advisory relationship.

Navigating Difficult Conversations

Sometimes, our clients get hung up on one or two of the

screens. Abortion is one example. Some of our Christian clients who have more-liberal-leaning views may worry about whether adopting a faith-based investment portfolio is compatible. We take a very grace-based approach. I will explain, for example, that while we do not invest in tobacco companies, we also do not invest in anti-tobacco. A client who chooses in his or her personal life to smoke cigarettes can still own a faith-based portfolio! After all, we are all sinners saved by grace! Regardless of your political view about the legality of abortion, I explain, "Would you really want to profit from that situation where a young mother is in crisis, making the most heart-wrenching decision of her life?" Even my most liberal clients can get on board with that and agree to avoid investment in the abortion industry without feeling they have compromised their political values. Of course, for the evangelical Christian with strong pro-life views, the abortion screen will be far more meaningful. But for non-believers or those with pro-choice political views, I have also found that the abortion screen is something they can tolerate.

Whom Will You Serve?

This leads to another important question. Whom will you serve? Will it be an all-Christian client base? Or more inclusive? We chose to be inclusive. As long as we make clear at the start of every relationship that all our advice flows from a biblical worldview and that we specialize in Faith- Based Investing strategies, our trust relationship grows from that foundation. I believe this approach presents an important opportunity to expose clients who would never darken the door of a church to God's love and the Gospel. This is who we are; this is what we do. Is that the kind of firm you are looking for? We can't be all things to all people, but we have an opportunity to create a client community that is special and grounded on biblical truth.

This was put to the test about three years ago when my firm acquired a practice from a retiring advisor. This advisor shared a strong faith and often prayed with his clients. However, he did not utilize Faith-Based Investing at the time, and only about 50% of his clients would self- identify as Christians. We were both taking a risk. He sought to maximize the value of his practice, and I was seeking to remain true to my vision and mission. Thankfully, the retiring advisor believed that introducing his entire client base to Faith-Based Investing would be an added blessing to those families and part of his departing legacy to them. We moved forward with the succession plan, and as a result more than tripled the number of families we served overnight. What a humbling moment that was for me. Two years later, the fact that approximately 90% of those families continue to invest with us is a testament to God's goodness and grace.

As a result of that succession plan, we now serve a very diverse practice—including families that would not self-identify as Christians, as well as some families that have alternative lifestyles. Did you catch that? Not all our advisory clients are Christians, but all of our advisory clients are invested in our faith-based models. How is this possible? I like to think it is because they trust me, enjoy working with me, and that we do a good job demonstrating God's love and compassion without judgment. This is the gospel of grace. If I made the decision to work only with clients who were without sin, there would be no clients! In fact, by the same measure, there would be no advisors! We are all sinners saved by grace. However, we are free to be reconciled to

God, love others, and honor and obey the best we know how in accordance with the Scriptures. It is a walk of humility seeking to reflect the light of Christ in this world, without pretense, judgment, or hypocrisy. Because of the work of the cross and the blood of Jesus Christ, we are saved!

Faith-Based Investing is an opportunity to extend the same heart of worship to investment choices that we already strive to apply to our relationships, spending, and giving decisions. It is just one more area where we have an opportunity to reflect God's love and compassion in the world. It is not a legalistic burden or obligation. The motivation for Faith-Based Investing should be one of joy and worship, not guilt.

To help clients grasp the heart story behind Faith-Based Investing, one tool we use for client investor education is my book, *Investing with Integrity: How Investment Choices Can Be an Act of Worship*. First published in 2014, the second edition was published in 2019. It is a client-facing book intended to be a light and entertaining read, especially for those who are new to the idea of Faith-Based Investing. I explain that this book is not intended to be a "how-to" book, but rather a "why does this matter" book. It addresses the heart-story behind Faith-Based Investing. Many other advisors have used the book as an investor education tool with great success, and the feedback I have received has been that clients find it enjoyable and helpful. To learn more or to order copies in bulk for your practice, visit www.investingwithintegrity.net.

"Then I heard the voice of the Lord saying, 'Whom shall I send? And who will go for us?' And I said, 'Here am I. Send me!'" (Isaiah 6:8, NIV)

Final Thoughts

I hope this chapter was an encouragement to you. If you feel the Lord calling you to develop a Faith-Based Investing practice, take courage. Surrender the decision to the Lord in prayer and seek godly counsel from trusted advisors. And, if you are married, make sure you have spousal unity. And may the Lord continue to bless you richly on your professional journey!

References:

1. Simon Sinek. (2009). Start with why: How great leaders inspire everyone to take action. New York, NY: Penguin Group.
2. Jim Collins. Good to great. New York, NY: HarperCollins Publishers.
3. Financial Industry Regulatory Authority. (n.d.). Key Statistics for 2017, FINRA, Retrieved from https://www.finra.org/newsroom/statistics

11

IMPLEMENTING FAITH-BASED INVESTING IN YOUR PERSONAL INVESTING

BY BRIAN COHOON

How Faith-Based Investing Is Making a Difference

I started in the investment business in 1992 when I was 22 years old. I remember vividly the first couple with whom I met for retirement planning. I was a brand-new licensed advisor with about two months of training. It was exciting and a little scary at the same time.

One of my early joys was working with a classic millionaire-next-door couple. The husband was retiring from Eli Lilly after nearly 40 years. They were a very pleasant and trusting couple. They spent less than they made over the years, raised a family, and were good savers. They now had over $1 million in a company retirement plan that was a big part of their new paycheck for the rest of their lives. They told me they came to me because they were nervous that they would make a big mistake and needed a trusted advisor to help them make smart money decisions. Now that was a lot of pressure to lay on a 22-year-old kid!

I immediately talked to two other Certified Financial Planner™ practitioners in the firm to learn from their experience and to get some guidance to help this couple who trusted me with their life savings. They guided me, and we developed a sound financial plan for them. I considered how many different options are available to clients in the financial and investment world. It must be paralyzing and hard to make sense of everything if you are not in this business on a daily basis. A few weeks after our meeting, I met with them and shared the financial plan, and they decided to move forward with me to manage all of their life savings. The comment the gentleman made to me in this meeting still resonates with me today: "We are here because we need your help. We trust you and will do what you tell us to do with our finances. If this is what you recommend as best for us, let's do it."

I remember thinking two things after this meeting. First, I can relate to their trust. I feel the same way in my own life when I take my car to a mechanic. I know my car needs attention, a thorough diagnosis, and a qualified technician to prepare my car for many more miles of traveling. I have no idea how to fix it. I trust that the mechanic is good and will charge me a fair price. In one sense, when I get behind the wheel again, my life is in that mechanic's hands. Second, after this meeting I developed a new goal for my client meetings: wouldn't it be awesome to find a way to analyze everything down to a "no brainer" situation for clients? I clearly saw the power that a trusted financial advisor has working with clients. I also saw the larger potential impact this can have for Kingdom causes when working with believers. I did not fully understand this for years. I'll come back to this "no brainer" thought and the impact that trusted financial advisors can have on Kingdom work a little later.

Early on in my career I was interested in what the Bible said about money. However, all the training that I received in the industry through my securities licensing and the Certified Financial Planner™ program and educational conferences never talked about incorporating faith with finances.

I operated for years under the premise that it is good to have a plan. It is biblical, and it is part of stewardship. I was providing advice and strategies to help people develop a sound plan and to be good stewards. My goal was to help them align their money and their life values. But for a believer, could this be expanded to align investment decisions for both the pursuit of financial returns and Kingdom impact?

Fast forward about 20 years, and I am now practicing as a financial advisor in Louisville, Kentucky. I joined a Bible study with other financial advisors who were exploring Scripture and discussing ways to incorporate their faith into important discussions in client meetings and investment portfolios. We studied Randy Alcorn's book *Money, Possessions, and Eternity*. It was in this study that I met a good friend and fellow advisor Dan Hardt. Dan is an independent advisor who was a pioneer in this field of thought. He had committed his practice to Christians who wanted to align their investment portfolios with their biblical values. Up to this point in my life, I never really thought about the effects of investments, both my clients' and my own. How were the mutual funds or stocks and bonds that I was recommending being used at the company level? How did these investments align with my personal values and, most importantly, with God's values?

At this time in the early 2000s, thought leaders were writing about the alignment of faith and investment. Technology was being developed to evaluate portfolios in a new way. A large movement was starting, and most advisors say that the term Environmental, Social, and Corporate Governance (ESG) investing started in about 2004. Many attribute that beginning to a letter from UN Secretary General Kofi Annan inviting over 50 CEOs of major financial institutions from around the world to a summit to find ways to integrate ESG investing into the capital markets. A year later this initiative produced a report entitled "Who Cares Wins."[1] The report made the case that embedding ESG factors into capital markets makes good business sense and leads to more sustainable markets and better outcomes for society. As I researched this initiative, I did not find anything anchoring it to biblical principles. This was a bit startling to me since the initiative used words like "embedding ESG factors into capital markets around the world." Think of the impact of that statement on society and the slippery slope of the "social" part of the ESG term if not anchored to biblical principles.

The ESG community was taking form, and I started to see this in my practice. Clients would approach me about the impact of their portfolios on the environment and would inquire if we could develop an investment program that was focused on companies that were favorable to the environment. The short answer was, yes, this was becoming possible. Global warming and climate change were the buzzwords. These principles were incorporated within investment policy statements for clients, and platforms were being developed to help advisors like me bring these investment solutions to clients who were concerned about ESG investing.

I remember working with one client who was focused solely

on protecting trees. This is noble, and I was not disagreeing with her that protecting trees is important. However, after pressing a little more, I learned that she was fine with profiting from companies that develop abortion drugs, sell tobacco and alcohol, or profit from pornography. Trees were her focus. This was shocking to me. I am not happy to admit it. But this was a large account, and I remember finding a solution for her to do just as she asked. We had a portfolio with companies that were favorable to trees and excluded companies that were unfavorable to trees. I stuck with this process, but I did not feel good about it. It became a regular part of my practice, like my desire at age 22 to find a "no brainer" approach for my retiring clients. I justified my tree portfolio because I had these new ESG tools to help her and really didn't have many tools to incorporate my faith or to share how avoiding companies that profit from abortion could possibly be a better investment for her. I was starting to see how people align their values to their valuables—however they define their values. For me as a Christian and as a trusted advisor, I needed to learn more about this topic. Is it possible to have a portfolio aligned for the pursuit of both financial returns and biblical impact? And could this be a "no brainer" that Christians and even non-Christians could embrace?

I was fortunate to spend two years working closely with Dan Hardt to help me answer these questions. Dan was utilizing some technology and some investment products that were focused on this very question. Here was the rub for me: I was trained to evaluate fees and performance on every investment, every time—period. I was also trained as a fiercely independent advisor who likes a flexible, open platform with many investment options for clients. If a mutual fund or investment portfolio costs more and you can see historically that it has lacked performance, you don't recommend this investment to clients for their life savings.

Let Me Take You Inside the Most Widely Held S&P 500 Index Fund (SPY)

Many investors are surprised to learn what activities they are profiting from and supporting through the companies they own in their investment portfolios. Below is an analysis of the practices reflected in the most widely held S&P 500 index fund.

S&P 500 Index Fund Values Analysis

Data sourced by lowpointinsight.com October 16,2018

Sources: 328,210,187 Americans, per the US census website (2018). Pew Research Religious Landscape Study (2018). Economic Policy Institute (EPI) - The Average American Family Retirement Savings (qualified money) is $95,776 (2016).

While we are here, let's also get a general understanding of the fees in portfolios. It is good to understand how investment product companies and advisors get paid to manage investments. This is oversimplified, and there may be more to consider in some scenarios (like individual stocks, etc.), but in general, there are fees both at the investment product level and for your advisor who is helping to professionally manage your portfolio.

Wall Street Average ($500,000 portfolio)

Fund Expense:	.68%
Advisor Fee:	1.00%
Total Cost:	1.68%

To my initial surprise working with Dan, I saw that clients at that time who were strong Christians and who saw charts like this above were quick to invest in faith-based mutual funds. They accepted some of the limitations on investment options and the possible sacrifice of long-term performance because their faith was strong. Using the term Faith-Based Investing (FBI) meant that they started with just that—their faith.

I am embarrassed to say it, but I was stubbornly looking for that "no brainer" and could not wrap my head around this as a good solution. I felt a sense of a judgment on clients too. On more than one occasion I tried offering this idea of Faith-Based Investing to clients as an alternative, and it came across as somehow judgmental in our discussions. This was most likely my fault in presenting it. When a client left after discussing FBI and not proceeding with that direction, I felt as if I had made them feel guilty if they chose to invest in a traditional manner. That was not my intention.

I also think this was part of my personal faith journey in this area. I resumed studying what the Bible teaches about money, and I read other books on this topic. My favorite book was Bob Russell's *Money: A User's Manual*.[2] This book helped me understand that the key to this entire journey is a change of heart, not a change in investment strategies. It inspired me to think of this as a heart issue, but I would be lying if I didn't say that I was still searching for the "no brainer" in this area.

During this same time, a verse that hit me hard was Proverbs 3:27: "Do not withhold good from those who deserve it when it is in your power to act." Wow, that is a tough one! Was I withholding good from those who deserve it by not sharing some of these investment options? Was I focusing purely on low cost and better performing investments, even in companies not aligned with biblical values? Is God not bigger, and does He not ask us to test Him in this area?

I am fortunate to be a member of a thriving church in Louisville, Kentucky. The mission of this church is to connect people to Jesus and to one another. Our senior pastor used an analogy of a dress shirt, and it stuck with me. He talked about getting that top button right—Jesus at the top. After that, all the other buttons fall into place. If that top button is off, every other button on the shirt is off, and the only way to fix it is to go back to the top button and get it right. Could this apply to investing as well?

About the same time that I started to think about this Top-Button idea, I met Robert Netzly. Robert recently started a disruptive faith-based investment firm called Inspire Investing. A new and fast-growing pioneer in this area, Inspire Investing is based in the San Francisco and Silicon Valley area. Inspire and other investment companies across the country are bringing new solutions to find these "Top Button" companies and provide solutions for clients of financial planners like me. Fortunately, today there are now many excellent, cost-efficient investment options available across the country to help advisors and their clients invest in line with biblical values. I noticed investment companies focused on endorsing positive companies and engaging negative companies to make changes. It was a nice positive approach and much different than the exclusionary approach of my past experiences.

I gravitated to this new way of framing the investment-decision process and of finding those companies that are a blessing. This helped me overcome that personal feeling I had in discussions years earlier when I felt this topic became judgmental and negative with clients. This was huge for me in my search for my "no brainer," and it also fit perfectly with this new idea of investing and getting that Top Button right.

Companies that are a blessing and are aligned with biblical values tend to perform above average when compared to firms that don't have that Top Button aligned to biblical values. Again, should I be surprised? Shane Enete, a Chartered Financial Analyst (CFA) and professor at Biola University, has shown that applying a biblical-values methodology to portfolio selection can actually generate outperformance in a portfolio when compared to broader, non-screened portfolios.[3] This was important validation that I needed in my journey. I now felt that I had new tools to share this concept with clients. It also helped me achieve peace, reconciling this new investment approach with over 25 years of secular training in this industry.

To make me feel even better on my journey, I learned about studies building on this ESG movement from a biblical perspective. In 2014 Oxford University reviewed 190 academic studies on the relationship between sustainability and firm performance. They found that 80% of the studies suggested a positive relationship between good sustainability practices and stock performance. And 88% of the studies indicated that the performance of firms was improved by strong ESG practices.[4]

Today, ESG investing is estimated to hold over $20 trillion

in assets managed in this fashion. This is around 25% of all professionally managed assets in the world! And it is rapidly growing still today with the help of the UN-backed Principles for Responsible Investment (PRI). PRI is a global initiative with over 1,600 member firms representing over $70 trillion in professionally managed portfolios around the world. PRI's stated mission is to advance the integration of ESG into analysis and decision making,[5] and many global exchanges now mandate ESG disclosures for listed companies. What an incredible impact from something that started with a simple visionary letter from Kofi Annan to 50 CEOs. Can all this success and momentum serve as a model for Faith-Based Investing as well?

In the past few years, research on Wall Street has expanded the ESG discussion, and Christian values are becoming part of the discussion. Studies at State Street Global's Project Delphi concluded, "Consideration of environmental, social, and governance criteria was once driven by ethical forces. Now investors are discovering how it plays a key role in broader financial performance and managing volatility."[6] Morgan Stanley stated in its recent research paper "ESG and the Sustainability of Competitive Advantage 2017": "We believe that ESG factors are integral to assessing the quality of a company and thus are a vital part of our investment process."[7]

Investment companies are taking notice, and "disruptors" are popping up in the investment industry. These new companies, disrupting the old order of values-neutral investing, are building on the ESG framework of the past 15 years. They are now developing low-cost investments such as exchange-traded funds that offer a broad selection of diversified investments aligned with faith- based values as options for advisors to share with clients. When these have been back tested, they show that they can actually improve investor outcomes. Wow—this could be my no brainer! Investing in inspiring companies aligned with biblical values, low fees, many qualified investment options (in fact, about 300 of the S&P 500 are qualified options) and the potential for above-average performance could be what I was looking for. This led me on my recent, more-intense 18-month journey to learn more about this area for myself and my clients. Maybe as an advisor and an investor I should trust God when He says, "Test me on this."

The Opportunity

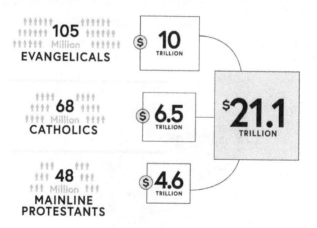

There is nearly $10 trillion in portfolios owned by Evangelicals living in the United States, $6.5 trillion owned by Catholics, and $4.6 trillion owned by mainline Protestants. This represents $21.1 trillion of investment assets owned by professing believers but are supporting abortion, pornography, and other activities that do not align with biblical values. Imagine the impact if we could align these portfolios with God's priorities. There are no excuses now for not knowing what you own. Online tools are available to x-ray your portfolio today if you wish.

If Christians began to discover what they were funding and made changes in their portfolios at larger levels, would corporations change their corporate actions? And what if we take it a step further? What if Christian investment firms also moved in this direction? What would it look like if individual Christian advisors used *investment company products* with a heart for giving with their clients *and* if whole advisory firms took this same approach with giving *at the advisor level?* This is a simple concept with exponential potential. See the gears grinding below. And to think ahead, new studies show that millennials are more actively engaged in this area than any generation previously.

Imagine the impact of giving at the product level and the advisory firm level. Imagine how this could unlock Wall Street for Kingdom impact! The gears illustration paints the vision of $100 million in assets aligned with investment product companies and advisory firms. These investments can conservatively generate $200,000 per year or more from current margins to fund Kingdom projects. If just one out of five (20%) of the Evangelical investors in the United States decides to make a portfolio change toward investment products and firms aligned in this manner, we are now talking about *billions* per year to fund Kingdom projects! Could this book have an impact similar to the 2004 letter from Kofi Annan?

Earlier in this chapter I mentioned the ability to "fund Kingdom projects." This is what really excites me today! These new disruptive companies are part of a growing movement of missional companies with a biblical worldview. These are for-profit companies working toward a purpose. So is it possible to unlock the potential of Wall Street and change Wall Street's culture and that of our world through some of these recent developments? Is it possible for this book to be like the letter sent to 50 CEOs in 2004? I believe it is possible and that God is moving in this space.

Could this book awaken investors to discover what their portfolios are funding and direct dollars away from a culture that profits from abortion and pornography? Could this also be a means of directing *wealth moving forward* to support inspiring, positive companies with for-profit investment and advisory companies? In this way these investment companies could use their businesses to fund projects such as Bible distribution in every language, offering the Gospel to all people groups in the world (visit www.joshuaproject. net) and developing more first-class, impactful Christian entertainment and media options for our children and for Kingdom impact?

So How Do I Do This?

If you are reading this as a financial advisor or an individual interested in investing in a manner that connects your values to your valuables, here is where I would suggest starting. Visit the website of Kingdom Advisors at www.kingdomadvisors.

com and hit the "Find An Advisor" tab to locate a financial advisor who has demonstrated professional competence and a commitment to biblically wise financial counsel. Many have also gone on to complete an additional level of training and expertise as a Certified Kingdom Advisor® (CKA). If you are a financial advisor, click on the "Become a Member" tab and learn how to incorporate biblical principles into your conversations with clients. This is the best place, in my opinion, to begin your journey of personally investing in this manner.

I shared that unlocking Wall Street excites me. Let me share why. I am the father to three awesome kids. As I write this, my son Brett is 22, and my beautiful daughters Paige and Maiya are 20 and 18, respectively. They have grown up with media all around them: movies, videos, iPhones, SnapChat, Twitter, Spotify, podcasts, Instagram, etc. I see firsthand the powerful effect of media on our youth. There is a battle for our culture, and it is being fought in media and technology.

One of my good friends is a godly, world-class businessman who is connected to the Christian entertainment industry. He had this vision long before I did. He is now experiencing tremendous success reaching lost people with the Gospel through film and other media. I am playing some catch up, but I see how my work in the investment industry and the power of media can intersect for a powerful Kingdom impact. Here is part of what I see now.

First-Class Christian Entertainment & Media

"Film is proving to be the most powerful, global way to tell Gospel-driven stories," according to award-winning filmmaker Jon Erwin of The Erwin Brothers and co-director of the recent hit movie *I Can Only Imagine*.[8]

First-class impactful films like *I Can Only Imagine* and *Hacksaw Ridge* are excellent examples of how these unlocked Wall Street fees discussed in this chapter can be efficiently invested for eternal returns and connect people to Jesus. *I Can Only Imagine* had a budget of less than $10 million, yet this film and others like it are highly acclaimed. How many of those could we fund each year if Christians simply reallocated their current investment portfolios with missional companies in the investment industry? These Academy Award-winning films are touching hearts and being recognized as quality products by the movie industry. The talent is in place with top filmmakers passionate to use film to tell these Gospel-driven stories. The demand for first-class movies is large and growing. There is a battle for our culture.

Conclusion

So is it possible to have a "no brainer"?

- First-class client experience

- Professional management

- Broad investment platform

- Investments in positive, impactful companies

- Competitive fees

- Competitive performance

- Alignment of your values to your valuables

- All of this—and unlock Wall Street for Kingdom impact

Yes, it is, and it took me many years to finally figure this out. But now I am convinced that we need advisory firms and investment product firms working together, and we can unlock Wall Street for exponential Kingdom impact.

Kyle Idleman, senior pastor at Southeast Christian Church, said it well in his great sermon series "SYNC: Aligning Your Resources with God's Priorities": "When what matters to God is what matters to you, every resource you've received can point others to Him."[9]

This is truly *wealth moving forward.*

Author Note: *I know that many great financial and investment advisors, people who provide excellent service to their clients, have differing opinions on Faith-Based Investing. Many Christian advisors also have differing opinions on Faith-Based Investing. This is fine. This chapter talks about my personal journey. My intent is not to judge but to point out the opportunity if Kingdom-focused advisory firms and investment product companies worked together to provide first-class investment services and to explore ways to use some of the Wall Street margins to spread the Gospel.*

References:

1. Who Cares Wins, (2004) Swiss Federal Department of Foreign Affairs & United Nations Global Compact

2. Money: A User's Manual by Bob Russell. Multnomah Books (April 1, 1997)

3.Performance Attribution of BRI, (2018) Shane Enete, CFA at Biola University

4.Oxford University,(2014), Sustainability Practices and Performance

5.www.unpri.org, Principles for Responsible Investment, Six Principles for Responsible Investment

6.State Street Global Advisor: Fall 2014 Issue

7. Morgan Stanley: ESG and the Sustainability of Competitive Advantage 2017

8. Motion Picture Association. (2016). Chairman's letter. Retrieved from https://www.mpaa.org/wp-content/uploads/2017/03/MPAA-Theatrical-Market-Statistics-2016_Final-1.pdf

9. Kyle Idleman, (2018), SYNC sermon series, Senior pastor at Southeast Christian Church

12

THE FUTURE OF FAITH-BASED INVESTING

BY HARRY PEARSON

Wayne Gretzky, one of the greatest hockey players of all-time, was asked what makes him so special. His response was, "I skate to where the puck is going, not to where it has been." While we wouldn't be here without the amazing contributions of those who've gone before us, we must move from "what is" to "what could be." Today, less than 1% of all assets stewarded by faith-based families are aligned with their values. Most are either unaware this is an option, aren't sure how to do it, or are concerned they'll have to sacrifice return for the sake of their values. The good news is now you don't have to choose. You can, in fact, make a great return, while also investing in companies that are aligned with what you value most.

Thankful to the Pioneers

I love the proverb, "We live in the shade of trees we did not plant." It reminds me of the ways God has used men and women who've gone before us to plow the ground, plant the seeds, and begin growing trees that produce fruit and shade. This whole concept of Faith-Based Investing (FBI) didn't just happen overnight. Over the past 30 years or so God has used men and women to question traditional ways of investing and to raise red flags at investments that didn't align with His principles. For this we are grateful for each person who has stepped out in faith, been courageous, and helped us get where we are today.

Great Message . . . Not the Best Delivery

Faith-Based Investing has had to evolve over time. Just like any new service or solution, it was clunky at the beginning, a little too expensive, and didn't produce the returns needed to be considered world-class.

Some of the early FBI solutions sort of remind me of Christian films 20 years ago. The message was always good, but the delivery wasn't best in class. It always felt like it was produced on a B rated budget. The film quality was the best they could do based on the resources they had, but it wasn't up to Hollywood standards.

Hollywood had more capital, more resources, could hire the best talent, do the biggest marketing campaigns, and really put on a show that everyone wanted to see. It's why they make the big money. People love being entertained. They love a great story, and they love feeling like they're seeing something done with the highest levels of quality. It's why they give out Oscars. The world recognizes and rewards the best of the best in the eyes of those voting. Have you ever seen a Christian-based film win an Oscar for Best Picture?

There are many reasons for that, but my point is that they never seemed to be best in class.

My point is simple. If we want to capture the attention of the world, we have to be world-class. We already have the best story. The good news of Christ should win every award. Our job, through His provision, is to allocate more capital and more resources, hire the best talent, do the biggest marketing campaigns, and really put on a show that everyone wants to see. A perfect example of this happened just this past year. The Erwin Brothers released *I Can Only Imagine* which took the nation by storm. Not only was the story great, but the quality of the film was incredible as well. When you combine a great story (the hope of the gospel) and a world-class presentation, the world will take notice.

Faith-Based Investing is no different. We must continue to grow and evolve for the world to take notice. There are many great FBI companies and investment solutions, but few have been recognized like Eventide. Eventide has found a way to be world-class, while also being grounded in biblical truth.

The world has taken notice. They have received some of the highest rankings by Morningstar and Lipper. They are cutting edge on process, people, and technology. They hire the best talent. They have a message that's attractive to all people. They deliver great performance. They are doing all the things needed to take market share, grow their footprint, and make a positive difference in the lives of those they serve.

It's time for others to follow suit. Many of the FBI firms are doing just that. They're hiring better talent, building better processes, and through the use of technology, beginning to execute in more cost-efficient, effective ways.

We See a Disconnect

Today, advisors manage a little over $40 trillion dollars on behalf of clients. Ten percent of that, or $4 trillion is stewarded by families of faith. Yet only $30 billion of that

$4 trillion is invested in a way that aligns with what those faith-based families say they believe. That means less than 1% of all money stewarded by families of faith is aligned with what they believe.

My first question is, why is that? After studying, researching, and asking hundreds of families, the three most common responses are:

- Most people are simply unaware

- Most aren't sure how to do it

- Many are concerned they'll have to sacrifice return

I'll address these three responses now.

Changed Lives . . . Change Lives

For years I'd heard of this concept called Faith-Based Investing. Quite frankly, every time I heard the words "biblically" and "responsible" in the same sentence all my legalistic past sort of flared up. When I heard people discuss it, I felt like it was presented as a dogmatic "you don't need to do this or that," or you need to avoid "the filthy five, sinful six, and nasty nine." I had this attitude: "Who are the guys in the black robes in the back room choosing what's biblically responsible or not?" I truly wanted no part of what I was hearing.

It wasn't until I had Eventide come speak to about 50 advisors that God began to change my heart. The speaker began his presentation by putting 17 mug shots on the screen. He said, "This was an escort service that was busted for prostitution in New York City. You'd expect the prostitutes and pimps to be arrested, but what about these two guys?" He hit a button, 15 mug shots went away, and there were these two faces left. He said, "These were the two guys that put up the money to start the business. What do you think happened to them?" He said, "Well, they were indicted just like the rest of the folks because the judge ruled that when you make an investment, you become an owner, and as an owner you have a higher level of responsibility." Then the speaker stepped up and said, "But the question is this. If an earthly judge will find these two passive investors guilty of how they invested their money, how will your Heavenly Father find you on how you've invested His?"

At that moment the question changed from "What is biblically responsible?" to "Who is the owner?" I had to conclude if He's the Owner then that makes me the steward. That led me to one simple question. As the steward, shouldn't I at least consider aligning His assets with His principles and with things that bless people instead of causing harm?

That was the moment that God graciously, gently, sort of popped me upside the head and got my attention. I knew at that moment that this was not just something I was going to think about, but this changed things. God opened my eyes to what He wanted me to see, and I was now aware and clear.

We came back home from that meeting and began buying books, software, and training on how to begin thinking through this process. I asked my team to take the 69 mutual funds and index funds we used to build portfolios and screen them to make sure they didn't have any revenue from abortion, pornography, or any gifts to Planned Parenthood. To my dismay, only three of our funds passed those three screens. That made me sad because I was clear that God wanted us to take action on this, but I couldn't put clients' money in three funds – a small cap fund, a healthcare fund, and a municipal bond fund.

We began to pray for the Lord to give us wisdom and direction. Psalms 127:1 says, "Unless the Lord builds the house, those who build it labor in vain." Wow! He really began putting the pieces together. I began to do research on the FBI space and found that it was all a bit confusing. Everybody had a little different definition of what they focused on. Some FBI firms were focused on shareholder advocacy. Some had a small definition on what to screen out; some a big, wide definition; and some seemed to align with a particular denomination.

I also noticed they all used different names to describe what they were about. Some used "biblically responsible;" others used "values based," "virtues based," "faith based," etc. I found that there were about 13 different definitions of this concept in investing. It was all quite confusing. The more I dug in, the more I found that many times the messaging was dogmatic and didn't seem loving and kind. That began a quest to figure out a better way.

As followers of Christ, we're tired of being told by the world that we're racist, bigots, unloving, unkind, etc., etc. However, unfortunately, many times this has been true. Our actions have been more focused on trying to change people's behavior instead of sharing the love of Christ which changes hearts. Instead of taking on the world through rules and protest, we must repent of our arrogance, pride, and self-righteous stances. In Matthew 5:3 Jesus reminds us, "Blessed are the poor in spirit, for theirs is the kingdom of heaven."

If we desire to change lives, we must begin the conversation from a place of humility—understanding and living out what it means to be poor in spirit. We're not here to teach and change people. We're here to simply share the Good News in a way that is attractive, uncompromising, and engages each heart that God places in front of us. Our job is to share; He does the rest.

Jesus gives another example:

"He also told this parable to some who trusted in themselves that they were righteous and treated others with contempt: 'Two men went up into the temple to pray, one a Pharisee and the other a tax collector. The Pharisee, standing by himself, prayed thus: "God, I thank you that I am not like other men, extortioners, unjust, adulterers, or even like this tax collector. I fast twice a week; I give tithes of all that I get." But the tax collector, standing far off, would not even lift up his eyes to heaven, but beat his breast, saying, "God, be merciful to me, a sinner!" I tell you, this man went down to his house justified, rather than the other. For everyone who exalts himself will be humbled, but the one who humbles himself will be exalted'" (Luke 18:9-14).

When I read this passage, it breaks my heart that I so easily hold others in contempt.

I so quickly judge by what I see and so flippantly, easily, say, "Lord, help those people...thank you that I'm not that way." I think he lets that come out of my heart, sort of like puss from a wound, so that he can take it, clean it up, and remind me of my sin. "Lord, help me be more like the tax collector who understood his place. He understood that he was completely dependent on you. He was clear that he was worse off than he could even imagine, but by your grace he was loved more than he could ever comprehend. Only by your mercy had he been set free."

This is how we must approach Faith-Based Investing. Only by His mercy do we understand that we have no hope apart from Him. Only by His mercy have our eyes been opened to the truth that He is the owner of all things, and we are the stewards. Only by His mercy do we get to share "that He sent His Son into the world not to condemn, but in order that the world might be saved through Him" (John 3:17). When we enter into dialogue with a repentant, humbled, kind, poor-in-spirit heart, this attitude allows that person to smell the sweet aroma of the Gospel, as opposed to the stench that's left when we boldly proclaim all that we believe to be right and wrong. A mentor encouraged me one time to do a whole lot more asking and a whole lot less telling. When we ask others what they value, it engages their hearts. When their hearts are engaged, it frees them to feel safe. When they feel safe, they can truly share their deepest desires.

As advisors, we have a privileged seat at the table. We get to sit knee to knee and enter into the lives of those sitting across from us. We get to hear their deepest desires, their joys, their sadness, their goals, and their greatest concerns. It is an honor and a privilege. We also have the opportunity to hold them accountable, helping them reach their highest and best intentions. Part of holding them accountable is helping them align their lives with what they say is most important. When it comes to investing, as stewards, we must help make them aware, so the Holy Spirit can do His work. We must be intentional and purposeful. In humility, we desire to be uncompromising on truth. We are not God, nor desire to attempt to play Him.

We do, however, have the Holy Spirit that guides us and goes before us. We have the power of Jesus in us. Many times, we as believers act more like the disciples pre-Pentecost. We stumble and fumble around with our words. We don't want to step on any toes. We use the excuse that we're all just broken people. And many times we fail to take a stand for that which God's Holy Word has made clear.

We don't have to keep putting on our old clothes. We have new clothes. We are a new creation. The disciples post-Pentecost did not deny Christ. They did not stand in the back letting the world just go on about its business. The same Peter that denied Christ before now stood and said, "You can beat me, but I'm going to share the Good News of Christ. You can kill my body, but I'm going to share the Good News of Christ. Do what you want, but I'm going to share the Good News of Christ. For apart from that Good News we have nothing." If our desire is to finish this life well, the only way to do that is to know and have a personal relationship with Jesus Christ the Savior of the world.

How Do We Change the Conversation?

When it comes to investing, we start the conversation by helping the client identify what they value most. We ask a simple question, "What values do you have that you would never want to violate just to make a profit?" They begin to name things that are most important, and we ask more questions to allow them to clarify why that is most important. At the end of that dialogue, they have typically named three to five values they would never want to violate just to make some return. We simply ask, "Do you know if your current investments are aligned with what you just said was most important?" Ninety-nine times out of 100 they say no. We say, "Would you like to?" And they say yes. We simply take their investments, identify anything that violates what they said, and give them recommendations on how to align their investments with their values.

Our simple goal is to take the best of what the world has to offer and to integrate biblical truth throughout the process. We start with the best portfolio managers. We all have a highest and best use. For advisors, picking all the right stocks and having the right tactical allocation is usually not it. There are world-class managers in every category. Just like a baseball team looking to find that ace pitcher, we're looking for that ace portfolio manager in large caps, small caps, international, etc. We then have a uniform screening process that is clear and simple to understand. All portfolio managers must adhere to our screening process and pick their top 40 or 50 best ideas in their particular asset class. We then take all of those and build an allocation that matches what the client said was most important.

Bob Doll is a perfect example. Bob is a devoted follower of Christ and is world-class in every way the world chooses to measure. When I shared that only three of 69 funds had passed the three screens making sure there was no abortion revenue, no pornography revenue, and no gifts to Planned Parenthood, he said, "I've never seen it like this before." I asked him, "Have you ever considered aligning your values with your investment expertise?" He said, "No, I've never had the opportunity to do that with the firms I've worked at." I said, "If you could, would you be interested?" He said, "Yes, that would be a dream come true." We began to pray through what that would look like and what needed to happen to make that dream a reality.

By God's grace, Bob is now managing OneAscent Large Cap

Core, OneAscent Large Cap Value, and OneAscent Large Cap Growth. For the first time in his career he is indeed aligning his deeply held values with his amazing skill, process, and investment expertise. We pray that this is just the start of showing the world that you can, in fact, make a great return while also living aligned with what you say is most important.

My prayer is that there are other Bob Dolls out there—incredibly skilled portfolio managers that would like the opportunity to do what they do best while at the same time making sure their investments align with the values they hold most dear.

Ready to Take the Next Step

If we're going to move the needle from 1% of all assets being aligned to faith-based values to 2%, 3%, 5%, or 10%, we must take action on building a preferred future. We must move from what is to what could be. That takes foresight. Foresight is the ability to predict what will happen or be needed in the future. Foresight is needed and used in many ways, but my purpose is to unpack what that might look like in the world of Faith-Based Investing.

What if you could invest with confidence knowing you had a solution offering world-class managers combined with world-class technology at a cost-effective price, all centered around a uniform screening process that allowed you to identify your values, and then align your investments to match?

If you knew that you could still make great returns while also helping humanity flourish, would that not inspire you to take action? I've not met too many people who don't want to make this world a better place as well as be a part of something that's bigger than themselves. In many ways this is a battle.

It's a battle for the hearts and minds of mankind.

In battle the flag bearer is one of the most important positions in a company. When the bombs start falling and the bullets start flying, it causes chaos. The soldiers get scattered and begin to look for the flag of their company to get reorganized, refocused, and reenergized to push forward again.

We also have a flag worth following. This world tries to knock us off course and get us distracted by all sorts of things. For investors, we've sort of been like sheep going down this path not fully knowing where we're going. The world has built all sorts of products and gotten us focused on returns instead of stewardship of what God has entrusted to us. Instead, we should consider the way the companies we're investing in make money. Are they filling a need, making a profit, and blessing mankind? Or are they filling a need, making a profit, and causing harm? Companies make money by selling a product or service. You should ask two main questions. First, are there any products or services that I want to make sure I don't promote or profit from? Second, what are the products and services I'd like to promote or profit from that are making a positive impact on the world?

You'll only ask these questions if you think like a steward who will be held accountable for how you managed the Owner's assets. This is both a responsibility and an opportunity to play a part in God's bigger story. By investing in, profiting from, and promoting companies that bring value to the world, you not only bring Him glory, but you also are using His assets to improve and impact the world.

I hope this has made you aware, informed you of how to do it, and shown you that you can indeed make a great return.

It's now up to you. Don't let this be just information that gets you excited but gets put on the shelf. I encourage you to take action. Identify what you value most. Align the assets you steward to match those values. Bless mankind. And bring God glory.

EPILOGUE: A CALL TO ACTION

BY BILL HIGH

"People don't buy what you do. They buy why you do it."

- Simon Sinek

I remember years ago watching the movie *Mr. Holland's Opus*. It's a touching story of a musician who dreams of writing and performing great music. But in view of reality, he gets a "temporary" gig teaching high school music. The gig stretches into years, and the story line follows Mr. Holland's ups and downs of teaching and engagement with various students. All the while, in his private hours, he works at music composition.

There's a question that hangs in the air throughout the movie: Will he return to his first love, writing music? But along the way, Mr. Holland learns that his greatest composition is the lives of the students he has invested in—they are his magnum opus.

I wonder if we will learn the same thing in the financial world. For years, it's been easy to pride ourselves in serving clients well, working toward great performance, and preparing people for retirement. The financial world is changing. Asset allocation strategies have largely become a commodity. Differentiation is harder. The statistics bear this out: The studies tell us that 66% of heirs will fire their financial advisors after their parents die.

What's the overt message from all this? We can get lost in the idea that our job is to make a financial product–that is, "to compose the music." But perhaps the reality is that we are crafting an opus in the lives of people.

What do I mean? As Mr. Holland learned, his opus was the lives of the students he taught. He helped his students realize who they were, the potential that existed within them, and how to live that out.

And I wonder if that's not the great calling of every individual: To discover our identity in Christ—truly loved, truly forgiven, truly called—and then to live out that identity in loving, serving, and giving in alignment with our values. I had one friend call it *the integral life*—a life in which all parts are integrated. It is the idea of a complete life where our values and actions are lived out together.

It seems to me that part of that integrated life extends to our financial world. Do we believe that God is a provider and giver? Perhaps we should give generously. Do we believe that God cares for the poor, the widow, and the orphan? Do our service and giving reflect that? Do we believe that God is a God of justice? Do we support mercy and justice?

In the same way, do our investment portfolios reflect the values we hold as believers in Christ. I'll be frank. My own walk has been a lifelong learning process. I've had to go back to my investment advisor and have him walk me through my portfolio to determine where that portfolio did not conform with my faith. We've had to make changes. Not all of these changes have been easy, but they have been good.

For me, I believe that this process of learning and change is helping me craft a better opus. That's our challenge—to grow, to investigate, and to keep discovering the opus that God is writing for us. May you continue to seek His will and His face as you consider investing by faith.

- Bill High

CEO of *The Signatry*

AUTHOR BIOS

ART ALLY is founder and president of the Timothy Plan. A former branch director for Bache Halsey Stuart Shields and Shearson-Lehman/American Express, Art founded Covenant Financial Management before launching the Timothy Plan in 1994. A devoted husband and father, author, speaker, businessman and advocate, he has worked for 40 years investing with Biblical standards. He helped found the National Association of Christian Financial Consultants, launched a tool to analyze mutual funds based on moral integrity (eVALUEator), wrote a workbook series on Biblical Stewardship, started the Liberty Pastors Network and is a founder of Reclaiming Florida for Christ.

BRIAN COHOON is a Certified Financial Planner practitioner, a Chartered Retirement Planning Counselor™, and an Accredited Investment Fiduciary™ who has been in that business since 1992. Over these years he has worked primarily with business owners, professionals, and individuals in their personal financial planning. He does extensive work with nonprofit organizations, endowment management, and volunteering. He continues his nonprofit consulting today with a fundraising consulting and charitable estate planning firm. As part of his career, Brian helped to create a financial planning department for a regional, publicly traded bank and developed and grew a territory in Kentucky for 401k and retirement plan business with a national trust company. He is a member of Southeast Christian Church in Louisville, Kentucky, and is a past board president of the Financial Planning Association of Kentucky.

STEVE FRENCH is president of The Signatry, where his primary role is strategic management and leadership of the office. He also devotes his time to meeting with advisors, attorneys, individuals, and business owners to develop strategies and solutions to minimize tax liability while maximizing charitable giving. This is executed with specific emphasis in the area of non-liquid assets such as stock, real estate, mutual funds, and portions of closely held businesses. Prior to joining The Signatry, Steve was the founder and CEO of Quovant, a legal spend management company working with law firms in over 13 countries. Steve and his wife Debbie have two daughters, Marnie and Rachel, who have blessed them with four grandsons.

LORAN GRAHAM is a Certified Financial Planner™ professional, a certified public accountant in Washington, and a Certified Kingdom Advisor®. Loran is passionate about making a positive impact in the lives of others. In his spare time, Loran enjoys the great outdoors, water sports, and creative writing.

BILL HIGH is the chief executive officer of The Signatry: A Global Christian Foundation. Prior to joining the foundation in 2000, Bill was a partner with Blackwell Sanders, LLP, a national and international law firm. He is also the founder of iDonate, a fundraising software company serving the nonprofit community. Bill invests his time working with families, individual givers, ministries, and financial advisors. He works strategically with business owners who desire to sell or transition their businesses to the next generation. He also teaches ministry leaders how to work with major donors. Bill's personal mission is to change the way people view and practice generosity, working with families to carry on a lasting legacy of true wealth. Bill has been married to his wife Brooke for more than 30 years. They have four children, two sons-in-law, and two grandchildren.

CHAD M. HORNING, CFA, is the president of Praxis Mutual Funds and senior vice president for Everence Financial, a leading provider of faith-based financial products in the United States and a ministry of Mennonite Church USA. As chief investment officer, he leads the investment team that manages corporate assets, client portfolios, and the Praxis Mutual Funds.

CASSANDRA LAYMON is the president of Beacon Wealth Consultants and LightPoint Portfolios. Cassandra holds a master's degree in adult education and an MBA, both from Rutgers University. She is a Certified Financial Planner™

and a Certified Kingdom Advisor®. She is a past leader of the biblically responsible investing special interest group for members of Kingdom Advisors. Cassandra is also the author of the book *I Found Jesus in the Stock Market: How Biblically Responsible Investing Can Change Your Heart, Too*. The book chronicles her quest to learn about honoring God with investments and how it ultimately led her back to her Christian roots.

RACHEL MCDONOUGH is passionate about helping people experience liberty and joy by integrating Christian values into their investment and financial decisions. She is a Certified Financial Planner™ professional and a Certified Kingdom Advisor® and loves to come alongside both investors and other financial advisors who want to put their faith into action.

JASON MYHRE is managing partner and director of marketing for Eventide, a Boston-based registered investment advisor practicing "investing that makes the world rejoice."® Founded in 2008, Eventide's vision is to serve individuals, financial advisors, and institutions by providing high-performance investments that create compelling value for the global common good. Learn more at www.eventideinvestments.com.

HARRY PEARSON is the CEO and co-founder of OneAscent. He has held many leadership positions in the financial services industry but is most passionate about empowering other Kingdom-building advisors to live out and fulfill their calling. With 22 years' experience, Harry incorporates his big-firm experience with the freedom and solutions needed to help families integrate their values with their investments, planning, financial stewardship, and generosity.

 MARK A. REGIER is vice president of stewardship investing for Praxis Mutual Funds and Everence Financial, leading provider of faith-based financial products in the United States and a ministry of Mennonite Church USA. Mark has been involved in the field of ethical and socially responsible investing at Everence for more than 20 years. He oversees the company's work in investment screening, ESG integration, proxy voting, corporate engagement and community development investing.

 JEFF ROGERS is the founder and chairman of Stewardship Legacy Coaching and Stewardship Advisory Group, one of the premier biblically responsible investment and wealth management firms in the nation. In 2013 Jeff was the recipient of the Larry Burkett Award from Kingdom Advisors, their highest award. He has over 35 years' experience in zero estate tax planning and multi-generational family legacy coaching. Jeff is nationally recognized for his expertise in strategic and tactical tax planning and charitable planning.

Jeff assists high-net-worth individuals and business owners in creating Kingdom capital by redirecting tax dollars to their favorite ministries. Jeff is the ForbesBooks-featured author of *Create a Thriving Family Legacy: How to Share Your Wisdom and Wealth with Your Children and Grandchildren.* He also co-authored *unPrepared: Heirs at Risk: 14 Elements for Successful Wealth Transfer* and authored the eBook *The Stewardship of your Business Legacy...Wisely Stewarding the Largest Financial Transaction of Your Life...Without Getting Killed with Taxes.*

DWIGHT L. SHORT completed more than 34 years as a financial advisor at Merrill Lynch, taking full retirement on August 3, 2005, having achieved the title of first vice president, investments and the Certified Investment Management Analyst® (CIMA) designation. Currently chair of the board for Christian Investment Forum, he has focused his retirement on missions, Faith-Based Investing, and grandchildren. He supports local Kingdom Advisor activities in the Tampa area, is part of the planning team for the CIF Leader's Summit and the missional outreach from St. James UMC, Tampa.

Dwight has authored three books: *Kingdom Gains: What Every Christian Should Know before Investing, Profit or Principles: Investing Without Compromise (the BRI story),* and *Home Is Where God Calls Us: Legacy of 20th-Century Missionaries and Their Students from Congo.*

JOHN SIVERLING is the managing partner in JAS Ventures, LLC, a consulting firm focused on helping companies develop and execute faith-integrated business practices. Following his lead role in the formation and launch of the Christian Investment Forum, a non-profit trade association, John became the first executive director in order to continue the growth strategy for CIF. The goal of CIF is to build awareness of and credibility for Faith-Based Investing within the broader financial investment industry. In addition to his work at the Christian Investment Forum, John is also a co-founder and president of Sentiens, LLC, an early-stage healthcare technology company. John holds a Bachelor of Business Administration Degree from the University of Wisconsin and an MBA with Distinction from the University of Michigan Ross School of Business.

HILLARY SUNDERLAND serves as the chief investment officer of Beacon Wealth Consultants and LightPoint Portfolios. She graduated magna cum laude from Bucknell University with a Bachelor of Arts degree in economics. She earned the Chartered Financial Analyst® designation in 2009 and the Certified Kingdom Advisor® designation in 2018. Shortly after graduating from college, she was deeply impacted through studying what God's word says about handling money and saw the need to take the message of stewardship, financial literacy and responsible investing to others. Hillary has co-led numerous small group studies focused on biblical financial principles and most recently was the co-founder of a firm focused on biblically responsible investing.